A Belief in People

A History of Family Social Work

"A belief in people, a belief in the complexity of each person, no matter how simple he may seem outwardly, a belief that each human being is different from all others and has a different contribution to make to this common living of ours, runs like a connecting thread through all the activities of the Association."

FRANCIS H. McLEAN

A Belief in People

A History of Family Social Work

Margaret E. Rich

FAMILY SERVICE ASSOCIATION OF AMERICA

192 LEXINGTON AVENUE   NEW YORK

Library of Congress Catalog Card Number: 56–12425

Printed in U.S.A.   *Price, $3.50*

To the memory of
Francis H. McLean

Foreword

It is with a sense of deep satisfaction that the Family Service Association of America presents this history of family social work. For many years the Association has been aware of the need for an authentic report of the origins and subsequent development of the family service movement, and the hope that such a history might be made available has been expressed many times, by both lay and professional persons.

The Association has always had a justifiable pride in the vital role played by the family field in shaping the pattern of social welfare in this country. Beginning as charity organization societies in the nineteenth century, these pioneer family agencies undertook to bring about reforms in methods of caring for persons in need. From the outset the leaders committed themselves to search for the causes of poverty and of human suffering, both in society and in the individual, and to endeavor to find new ways of reducing social evils as well as new ways of helping persons and families in distress. These two endeavors were viewed as complementary, with one reinforcing the other.

This dual approach, which has characterized family social work throughout its history, led to the development of two major social work methods—community organization and social casework. In this volume, Miss Rich traces the work of early family agencies in both spheres, describing the new principles and techniques that emerged and their impact on social work development and on social work education.

Margaret E. Rich was eminently qualified to write the history of family social work. Numerous persons over the past ten years put forward the suggestion that the Association arrange with her to write its annals. In fact, the suggestion came from so many quarters that it is not possible to give credit to the person or persons who gave impetus to this project. When Miss Rich was first asked to undertake the assignment she felt unable, because of other commitments, to devote the necessary time to the research that would be entailed. She was receptive to the idea, however, and agreed to begin work on the book at a later date. Since 1952, Miss Rich devoted most of her time to this project.

Miss Rich completed the work on the manuscript only a few weeks before her death, on May 6, 1956, in New York City. The Board of Directors of the Association, as well as many other friends and former colleagues, deeply regret that she did not live to see her book in print. We are all grateful, however, that she was able to complete the arduous task of assembling and organizing the material, and of writing this detailed report. She worked patiently and painstakingly, searching the archives and reading countless documents, with unflagging interest and with determination to produce an authentic history.

Except for a few years, Miss Rich spent her entire professional life in the family service field, beginning her career in 1909 as a caseworker in the Boston Associated Charities. She later became a district secretary in that agency, and from 1915 to 1918 she was director of the Newton family agency.

For almost twenty years—from October, 1919, to December, 1938 —she was a member of the staff of the Association, serving in many capacities and holding the position of assistant general director. During the greater part of this period, she was also director of publications and editor of *The Family* (now *Social Casework*). This journal, from its beginning in 1920, was intended as a medium of exchange not only for social workers in the family field but for those who were endeavoring to apply the newly formulated principles of casework in other settings. When Miss Rich joined the editorial staff, first as associate editor and later as editor, *The Family* was in its first year of publication and had only a handful of subscribers. In the next two decades, *The Family* became a major social work publication, read and studied by social workers and students the country over.

From 1938 to 1948, Miss Rich was director of the Family Society of Allegheny County in Pittsburgh, and during part of that time served as a member of the Board of Directors of the Association. From 1948 to 1952 she headed the Social Work Vocational Bureau in New York. During her career, Miss Rich taught at several universities and schools of social work and was the author of a number of articles and pamphlets.

The Association would like to acknowledge its deep debt of gratitude to Margaret E. Rich for her many services and for writing this volume. It would also like to acknowledge with thanks the contribution made by the Community Service Society of New York in helping to underwrite this project. The Association's contribution came from funds left to the organization by Francis H. McLean, its first director.

CLARK W. BLACKBURN
General Director
Family Service Association of America

October 1, 1956

Preface

IT IS ALMOST fifty years since I was introduced to charity organization and to the high adventure of social casework, when the Boston Associated Charities, then thirty years old, took me on as an apprentice worker. Zilpha D. Smith, who had been the society's first general secretary, had resigned several years before to serve as associate director of the Simmons College School of Social Work, but she was very much in the picture when I began to supervise students in 1910. So too were a number of others who had been active in starting the agency and who still served as friendly visitors and board members. It was from these friendly visitors and volunteers—I had nearly one hundred in my district—as well as from the paid staff that I absorbed some of the principles on which the work was based and learned that in working with people there could be no rule of thumb, no uniform procedure.

It was my dream for many years to write a history of charity organization by telling the story of each society—its origins, its program, and its activities—at various stages in its development. Only so, I felt, could I present the complexities and diversities of these societies and give an accurate description of this "new charity." The salient feature of these societies was the individuality of each. No two were alike, in origin, in program, or in growth.

v

Obviously, the task of gathering such extensive material was not practical, so I have had to content myself with giving illustrations of the beginnings and activities in a few cities. Incomplete as this report is, I hope that it succeeds in conveying the idea of diversity and individuality. Charity organization did not advocate specific methods. D. O. Kellogg, in the early periodical *Lend a Hand,* described it as "the embodiment of a spirit bent on finding effective methods."

In a sense, charity organization—or what we today call family social work—had no definite beginning. It was deeply rooted in the past and, as George B. Buzelle said at the National Conference of Charities and Correction in 1892, "its principles are as old as the mutual needs and mutual obligations of society." The idea of forming such societies occurred in the minds of many, although the name and the exact structure remained nebulous.

Helen Bosanquet has pointed out that it is difficult to be definite about the individual or group finally responsible for launching the London Charity Organisation Society in 1869 and that "if it had not been one, it might well have been another." This same sense of inevitability was expressed in various ways in the United States. At the 1883 National Conference of Charities and Correction, J. W. Bachman, one of the founders of the society in Chattanooga, said, "It strikes me as a very significant fact that this work of organizing charities has pressed itself upon so many minds and hearts, in so many places, at or near the same time." Many charity organization leaders have reminded us of the debt owed to such religious leaders as Frederic Ozanam, Thomas Chalmers, and Joseph Tuckerman; also to the St. Vincent de Paul societies, to the societies "for preventing pauperism," and to the associations "for improving the condition of the poor." Charity organization began, in the words of Mrs. James T. Fields, one of the Boston leaders, not hurriedly, but "as an intelligent outgrowth from old methods which were leading to no good end."

The development of these early societies was uneven; some grew steadily while others withered for a time and later put forth new shoots and thrived again. But even in the worst years of a society, some patient and thoughtful work was done by a few persons which often led to new growth.

In this brief story of family social work, I have tried to show this diversity both in its beginnings and in its growth. I remember vividly my surprise when I went to Mary E. Richmond's Institute in 1915 and discovered that Cleveland, New York, Minneapolis, Chicago, and other cities were different from Boston, not only as cities but in the methods and programs of their societies. I came to know more of this diversity when I became executive of a small agency and later when I was on the staff of the Association.

Because of the individuality of agency programs, particularly in the early years, it has not been possible to present the material in neat, chronological order, describing the characteristics of the work at certain periods. Charity organization development did not follow an even course and therefore does not fall into definite "periods." The efforts of the early societies in working toward various social reforms were highly individualistic and there was a wide variation of opinion among the leaders about ways of achieving certain ends. Along with their social reform activities, these societies were endeavoring to understand and help troubled persons and families as well as to train volunteers and staff for the task. These efforts, too, were individualistic and followed no set pattern.

In the first five chapters, I have tried to show the diversity of the programs of some of the early societies and the range of their activities. These chapters overlap in the time covered; they start with the beginnings of charity organization in this country in the 1870's and continue into the early decades of this century. The subsequent chapters are organized chronologically and describe major trends during certain approximate periods, ending with 1955.

I had hoped to include some biographical material about persons who played an active part in forming and guiding the various societies. This idea also proved too ambitious and had to be set aside. Miss Richmond once named, as the great pioneers of the charity organization movement in this country, four persons: Robert Treat Paine of Boston, John Glenn of Baltimore, Josephine Shaw Lowell of New York, and Oscar C. McCulloch of Indianapolis. This list is far from complete. Obviously, Miss Richmond herself should be on the roster. I should also add: Zilpha D. Smith of Boston, Gertrude Vaile of Denver, Mrs. John M. Glenn of New York, who was president of the Association from 1920 to 1936, and Francis H. McLean, the Association's first director.

I am deeply grateful to the Family Service Association of America and to the Community Service Society of New York, the two organizations that have made this venture possible financially. I owe my heartfelt thanks to the many individuals who have given me help in my search for material, many of whom sent me letters and documents from their personal files. Among those who have been particularly helpful are: Bertha Bayer, who has charge of the archives at the Community Service Society of New York; Mrs. Mary D. Paasch, librarian at the Family Service Association of America; Mrs. Margaret M. Otto and her colleagues at the library of the New York School of Social Work, Columbia University; and Stiena Elizabeth Benson, librarian of the Simmons College School of Social Work.

I owe a special debt of gratitude to Cora Kasius and to Shirley Moore Martin of FSAA Publications Service for their encouragement, help, and patience.

MARGARET E. RICH

April 1, 1956

Contents

CONTENTS

A Belief in People

A History of Family Social Work

I. Beginnings

FAMILY SOCIAL WORK in the United States had its beginning when the first city-wide charity organization society was started in Buffalo in 1877. Four years of civil war, followed by a nation-wide depression in 1873, had increased the number of unemployed, and misery and destitution seemed almost to feed and multiply upon the indiscriminate almsgiving of charitable agencies and individuals.

Conditions in Buffalo were no worse than in other large cities; certainly not so bad as in New York City or even in Boston, where a devastating fire had wiped out the heart of the business district. But in Buffalo there was a group of young men who were deeply concerned about the increase in "pauperism"—a word that was frequently used both in a legal sense and to designate chronic dependency or merely poverty. They were concerned not only about the conditions resulting from the war and the depression but also about the well-meant though ill-advised attempts to relieve distress by the giving of alms. Year by year there was an increase in the number of people receiving relief from the city "poor" department, in the number of tramps who went from house to house and beggars who accosted people on the street. The young men were convinced that something could and should be done to bring order out of this philanthropic chaos and to rescue the poverty-stricken from themselves and from their would-be benefactors.

The answer to their problem was supplied by the Rev. S. Humphreys Gurteen who had recently come from England to Buffalo to serve as associate rector of St. Paul's Cathedral. Mr. Gurteen was familiar with the work of the London Charity Organisation Society which had been started in 1869 to remedy conditions similar to those in Buffalo and in other cities in this country.[1] He suggested that Buffalo follow London's example and he paved the way for public understanding and support by a series of Sunday evening sermons on "Phases of Charity"—sermons "designed to bring the important subject of the organization of our city charities to the attention of our citizens." Each sermon was printed in a local newspaper and later his five lectures were published in a pamphlet along with a plan for organizing a society.

Gurteen incorporated this material in *A Handbook of Charity Organization* to serve as a guide in regulating the aid given to individuals and families in distress: applicants should work for any help they received; regular employment should be found for them when possible; instead of alms, loans without interest should be arranged; to help the poor help themselves was preferable to doing things for them; best of all was to make provision to prevent their falling into distress. Above all he urged the protection and strengthening of the home, including provision for better housing and social and sanitary reforms. He pointed out the need for intelligent co-operation of all classes, and of private charitable agencies with official relief bureaus. He recommended exchange of information and free transmission of cases from one to the other as private or official relief seemed more suitable. One basic principle was underlined: the complete severance of the work "from all questions of religious belief, politics and nationality." [2]

In support of his proposal Gurteen quoted from some of the individuals whose work and ideas had influenced the development of the London society. Among them was Edward Denison, who had lived and worked among the London poor and believed that "all bodily aid to the poor is a mistake and that the real thing is to let things work themselves straight; whereas by giving alms you keep them permanently crooked." [3] Another was Octavia Hill, who, in her work for better housing for the poor in London, had demonstrated the value of volunteer visitors trained to "develop

4

the resources of the poor themselves, instead of letting them come upon the rates, or continue upon them." [4] Gurteen was also influenced by Thomas Chalmers, a Glasgow clergyman, who had tried out successfully a plan to help his parishioners develop their own capabilities rather than depend on economic relief. Gurteen was especially enamored of Chalmers' plan (although it did not originate with him) to "bridge the chasm between the rich and the poor" by dividing an area into manageable sections under responsible visitors, who would "come into actual contact with the dwellings of the extremely poor." [5] The plan finally adopted for the Buffalo Charity Organization Society and put into operation in December, 1877, was an adaptation rather than a copy of the London plan. As T. Guilford Smith, one of the agency's founders, said a few years later:

> Cities differ so much from each other, that it is very difficult to say just how it is best to start a charity organization society, but in Buffalo we found that we made a success mainly by departing from the London model in one important particular, though following it in almost all others. That was, in starting first our Council and our Central Office. [6] [In London the districts had been organized first.]

Although the charity organization movement was "the first attempt to organize all existing charitable relief agencies into a working whole for the better division of labor and the more effective aggregation of effort," [7] it owed many of its distinguishing features to earlier efforts on behalf of the poor and the underprivileged, to the forerunners who had tried out one or more of the principles that the new societies now undertook to put into practice and to work out consistently in one program. In Germany, some of the principles in the administration of municipal relief had been applied first in Hamburg in the eighteenth century, later in Elberfeld and other cities. Frederic Ozanam in Paris, like Chalmers in Scotland, had seen the importance of "alms of good advice." In 1833, Ozanam, then a law student in Paris, joined with other young men to serve God "in the persons of the poor whom they were to visit at their own dwellings and assist by every means in their power." [8] This was the beginning of the St. Vincent de Paul Societies which have become international in scope.

In this country, the Society for the Prevention of Pauperism, started in New York City in 1817, incorporated many of the purposes and principles of the charity organization movement but within a few years it abandoned its attempts to prevent pauperism and devoted its energies to the prevention of juvenile delinquency. In 1834 Joseph Tuckerman, a Unitarian minister, set up an Association of Delegates from the Benevolent Societies of Boston with provisions for personal service and co-ordination of relief through central registration of the names of relief recipients but this project, too, proved to be short-lived. The Associations for Improving the Condition of the Poor—the first of them started in New York City in 1843—undertook to remedy the same kind of conditions which had faced the Society for the Prevention of Pauperism in 1817 and which the charity organization societies were to attack in the 1870's. The First Annual Report of the New York AICP, in 1845, shows that these Associations, too, were concerned about such problems of organization and method as lack of discrimination in relief giving; charitable societies' acting independently of each other; no adequate provision for personal intercourse between benefactors and recipients of alms; no provision for removal of the causes of pauperism. Similar associations, some using the same name as the one in New York, some, as in Boston, known as Provident Associations, were organized in a number of cities in the United States and in Great Britain. Many of them did notable work in sanitation, housing, and health education. The Boston Provident Association undertook to foster co-operation by a Charities Building, erected in 1869, to house both municipal and private charities. For the most part, however, meeting the demands for relief eventually crowded out most of their other activities.

In other isolated attempts to improve conditions some communities adopted the ideas of charity organization before the Buffalo Charity Organization Society was launched. The Germantown Relief Society, organized in 1873 in a suburban ward of the city of Philadelphia, followed the pattern of the London Charity Organisation Society. In 1874, a Bureau of Charities in New York City started a registration service but it failed to gain co-operation and was active only for a year or so. In 1875, the Society for Co-operative Visiting Among the Poor was founded by a group of women in Boston, influenced largely by the writings of Octavia Hill. The following year a group of volunteer workers in Boston, headed by

6

Frances R. Morse, started a registration bureau modeled on the one in New York.[9] All these agencies applied the charity organization principles but their efforts were partial, either in the area covered or in the scope of activities undertaken. They seem to have had little influence on the later development in Buffalo of a city-wide society prepared to undertake all the responsibilities implicit in organizing charity.

The Early Societies

During 1878, the year following the organization of the Buffalo society, five other cities—New Haven, Philadelphia, Brooklyn, Orange (New Jersey), and Syracuse—established charity organization societies. In 1879, societies were established in several other cities, including Boston, Indianapolis, Detroit, Cincinnati, Newport (Rhode Island), Portland (Maine), and Poughkeepsie (New York).* Although the objectives of these organizations were generally similar to those of the Buffalo society, there were a number of differences in the form of organization.

New Haven, a university city with a population of about 60,000, was on the main line between Boston and New York and was therefore an attractive stopover for vagrants. The number of vagrants in consequence was out of all proportion to the city's size; according to one report the number was exceeded only in Philadelphia and Cleveland.[11] Members of the Yale faculty were among the sponsors of the agency, which was designed primarily, although not exclusively, to take care of the problem of "trampery"—as it was sometimes called. The Organized Charities Association of New Haven, which started its work in May, 1878, was literally an association or federation of six relief agencies. Later it became similar in form to other charity organization societies.

Philadelphia took its first step toward organizing charity in 1876, two years before the plans were completed. In 1876 a number of prominent citizens met to consider some plan for improving the

---

* Authorities differ on the exact dates of the organization of the early societies. The information given here is derived from the article, "Charity Organization in the United States," based on a questionnaire prepared by a National Conference committee of which Charles D. Kellogg, general secretary of the New York Charity Organization Society, was chairman.[10]

7

distribution of alms by the 270 charitable agencies of the city. Much educational work, and much placating of agencies jealous of their prerogatives, had to be carried on by the organizing committee before an acceptable plan was arrived at. The Rev. Day Otis Kellogg, one of the organizers and the first executive of the society, later wrote that but for the divergence in views and need to reconcile conflicting plans, Philadelphia would have been organized earlier than Buffalo.[12] Finally launched in 1878, the Society for Organizing Charitable Relief and Repressing Mendicancy soon shortened its name to Society for Organizing Charity. The new agency, influenced by the representatives from the Germantown Relief Society who served on the committee, followed closely the London pattern, with district committees in each ward electing the Central Council. In practice each of the thirty ward committees was, for many years, an independent society with only a very tenuous relationship to the Central Council.

In Brooklyn, which was then an independent city, an organization meeting took place in November, 1878, and in January, 1879, the Bureau of Charities began operations. A group of volunteer visitors, who had been appalled by the abuses they found when visiting applicants for public outdoor relief, provided the impetus for this new organization. Prominent among its advocates was Seth Low, who became its first president. The Bureau was designated as a clearing house, modeled on the one set up in New York City in 1874. In 1882, the Bureau assumed additional functions and became a charity organization society in all but name, with special emphasis upon employment.

In Boston, the sponsors of the Registration Bureau and of the Co-operative Society for Volunteer Visiting Among the Poor joined in setting up an organizing committee which, after a year and a half of active propaganda, established the Associated Charities in December, 1879. This incubation or propaganda period, usually of some length, between the inception and the culmination of a plan for a society, gave opportunity for interpretation of what was meant by charity organization and was one of the strengths of the movement, since it ensured that the agency was strongly rooted in the community. The choice of a name for the Boston agency was felt to have been helpful in fostering friendly relations between the other societies. In a report for the agency made by a committee of board members including Erving Winslow, Ellen S. Hale, and Charles P. Putnam, in 1883, this comment appears:

> The fact that we are on such generally friendly terms with all the important societies we believe to be due to our having started with the idea of drawing these societies toward each other and of aiding them to organize their work rather than with the idea of organizing them from outside—as "Associated Charities" rather than as a "Charity Organization Society." [13]

As evidence that it was to be an "association of charities," the governing body was made up of two hundred delegates representing the charities of the city. This proved too clumsy an instrument for administration and was soon abandoned as were similar devices in other cities. Actually the Associated Charities in Boston and elsewhere adopted the principles of the charity organization movement, if not the name. At the insistence of the Boston Provident Association, the new society agreed to give no relief from its own funds. This decision, together with the emphasis on friendly visitors already enlisted through the Co-operative Society, was an important factor in keeping the focus of the agency's work on needs other than material.

In New York City, where conditions were worse than anywhere else in the country, the first attempts to organize concerted action were met with hostility, suspicion, and almost complete lack of co-operation. The New York State Charities Aid Association, under Louisa Lee Schuyler, tried repeatedly to arouse interest in some plan for organizing the charities of the city. Open meetings—with speeches by Humphreys Gurteen of Buffalo, Robert Treat Paine, president of the Boston Associated Charities, and others, including Miss Schuyler herself—and even the support of the United Hebrew Charities, which had been established in 1874 on charity organization lines, made no impression. Finally, in 1881, the problem was placed before the New York State Board of Charities. Josephine Shaw Lowell (Mrs. Charles Russell Lowell),[14] a member of the State Board, acted as spokesman for those who realized that something must be done. She presented a statement of conditions in the city based on such figures as she was able to collect about the number of people receiving alms and the amount of money being spent—"half a million dollars distributed annually to half a million people"—and requested the Board to appoint a committee, composed of its New York City members, with authority to devise some remedy. Except for this formal backing by an outside agency, which was an unusual procedure, the New York Charity Organization Society followed the usual plan in getting under way, with a local group taking responsibility for the various necessary steps. Its organization, one of its board members said, was "entirely the reverse of what it has been anywhere else, but the only way it could be done in the city of New York." [15] The society began work in April, 1882. So strong was the conviction of its sponsors that almsgiving would interfere with their real objectives, the constitution had a clause forbidding the society to give relief from its own funds.

By 1883, some system for organizing charity had been established in 28 cities; by 1892, the number had increased to 84, with the majority north of the Potomac and east of the Mississippi. Many others had come into being but were short-lived. They had been started with "too great enthusiasm at the first; an ignorance of the principles of the new movement. The expectation of early results was too large; the patience with fellow-workers was too little." [16]

Organizational Steps

Although there was no fixed pattern, most of the societies followed more or less similar procedures in getting an organization under way. The handbook written by Gurteen served as a guide for many years but it was not followed slavishly. First, as in Buffalo, a group of citizens interpreted the need and the plan to as many members of the community as they could reach; they drafted a constitution and in general set the wheels in motion. Later this group of sponsors, with the addition of others who shared their convictions, became the supporting membership of the society. The membership chose a board of directors to serve as the governing body. The board responsibilities included selecting staff—with one person, who was usually paid, named as executive—and advising on the activities of the agency.

In the larger cities the societies were districted, following Chalmers' plan of "manageable sections." Each district had an office—

10

usually in charge of a paid "agent" or worker—a corps of volunteer workers, and a district or case committee. This committee undertook to consider the needs of applicants and the particular problems of the neighborhood, and to promote co-operation between agencies. In the smaller cities, where districts were not necessary, there was one case committee instead of several. In both large and small communities, committees on special projects were appointed as the need for them arose. Rarely did a city copy without change the structure and activities of a society of another city, no matter how successful the work of the one society may have been. Diversity, not uniformity, was considered desirable "as enlarging the number of experiments tried and as throwing side-lights upon special problems." [17] The principle of individuality had free play as long as the main principles of charity organization were adhered to. As the Rev. J. W. Bachman, a board member of the Chattanooga Associated Charities, said in 1893: "We kept the plan [of other cities] just as much as we thought was good for us." [18]

Efforts to learn what others were doing began early. The Second Annual Report of the Boston Associated Charities makes this clear:

> The societies springing up everywhere show that other cities feel the need of some preventive and curative work that reaches farther than the immediate crisis of distress and that the method we have adopted commends itself to them. Representatives from charity organization societies in Philadelphia, Brooklyn, Buffalo, Cleveland, Washington, New York, Syracuse, Taunton, Pittsfield, Lowell, and London, and persons desiring to start similar associations in Baltimore, Montreal, Cambridge, and Quincy, have examined our methods personally during the last year, while with others we have had mutually helpful correspondence. A copy of each of our publications is sent, as issued, to one hundred and twenty-seven persons in 66 cities and towns. From many of them we receive reports in return, and we find them willing and eager to help us by investigations and co-operation of every sort.

In addition to personal visits and correspondence, leaders of the societies found opportunity for a free exchange of ideas at the yearly sessions of the National Conference of Charities and Correction, later to become the National Conference of Social Work. In its early years (1874–78) the Conference met under the auspices of the American Social Science Association. In 1879, the Conference became an independent body, and appointed a Committee on Charity Organization. The members of the first committee were Joseph Perkins, Cleveland; Seth Low, Brooklyn; Oscar C. McCul-

loch, Indianapolis; S. Humphreys Gurteen, Buffalo; G. C. Truesdale, Chicago; and Dr. O. W. Wright, Milwaukee. The committee
was continued for many years under various names and became a
regular section of the Conference.

The report of the first committee was made in 1880 by the Rev.
Oscar McCulloch, pastor of Plymouth Church in Indianapolis, a
forceful leader and an advocate of organized charity from 1878 to
his death in 1891, "a sort of missionary bishop of the gospel of
Organized Charity to the Middle West." [19] His report was a mas-
terly summing up of the philosophy and aims of the charity organization movement. Subsequent committee reports dealt with the
state of charity organization from year to year and gave accounts
of activities, successes, and failures of local societies. In 1887 the
committee devised a statistical card—the first of many—which was
to make it possible to have comparable statistics from the different
societies on the causes of poverty and the number and types of
problems dealt with. The section programs included papers by
volunteers and paid workers on the day-to-day work of the societies
and there was always time for free and vigorous discussion. The
International Congresses of Charities, especially those held in Paris
in 1889 and in Chicago in 1893, still further broadened acquaintance and stimulated experimentation. The printed proceedings
of the National Conferences and reprints of many papers were of
very practical value in giving the societies, widely separated geographically as they were, the strength that comes from belonging to
a movement with at least a semblance of common ideals.

Neither "charity organization" nor any of its variants was a very
happy choice as a name for the new movement. Mrs. Lowell of the
New York society expressed her own dissatisfaction, a dissatisfaction
probably shared by many of her colleagues, when she said:

> I do not like the name we have chosen, because "charity" means, in
> common speech, some kind of help given to "the poor"; and I wish we
> could find a name which would cover the idea of good done to the
> whole community, to the doers, as well as to others. I should very much
> like it if some idea of good citizenship, and of the duties done by, and
> for, citizens in mutual service, could be embodied in our name. "Organ-
> ized charity" is very limited, and does no justice to the aims of the
> societies we represent.[20]

The name did, to be sure, embody the idea of order and system,
sadly needed in the confused efforts to help the "poor"—a word that

12

the new charity used apologetically "for want of a better"—but it suggested a mechanical rather than a human approach and failed to make clear that the societies were concerned with the family as the "civic unit" and that all their undertakings were related, directly or indirectly, to protecting and strengthening the home. It was to be many years before the term "family service" came into use but from the earliest days "work with families" was the phrase charity organizationists used to describe what they did in behalf of those who sought their help.

In addition to having a strong belief in the need for order and for system and kindliness in meeting human need, the men and women who started the charity organization movement were convinced that there was a science of charity, that poverty could be cured and could be prevented because it was a result of causes that could be discovered and be removed. Through scientific charity it would be possible to "cure the misery of those who suffer now, and work constantly toward such improvement in circumstances that the number of the miserable shall diminish day by day." [21] They believed that these ends were to be achieved by scientific methods, by intelligent action founded on definite and thorough knowledge of the facts, whether to help the individual find a way out of his difficulties or to help the community improve its charities and reform its social conditions.

The new charity was a protest—and a strong protest—against the lack of factual knowledge which characterized so many of the philanthropic undertakings of the time. The new charity believed that wholesale and indiscriminate relief giving was injurious and uncharitable and that the giver had a responsibility for the effect of his gift. But the movement was much more than a protest. Its aims embraced not only knowledge and order and system but a more abundant life for the individual—better wages, better working conditions, and some of the pleasures of living. In a letter to her sister-in-law, in 1883, Mrs. Lowell said, "I more and more feel, the more I see of these suffering people, that things are all wrong. It cannot be right that men should slave all their days for bread and butter. They do need time for some amusement, or at least for rest, and they do need money enough for their labor to enable them to lay by for a sick time or for old age without giving up all that makes life worth living." [22]

13

If the all-embracing aims of charity organization were to be achieved, a broad program was called for—a program involving four major and, to some degree, interdependent areas of activity: to bring about co-ordination of effort and co-operation among charitable agencies and individuals; to demonstrate the value of discrimination and adequacy in relief giving; to change community conditions that were causing poverty and distress; and, as Mrs. Lowell said, to "bridge the chasm between the fortunate and the most unfortunate" by that "truest of all charity, personal interest in persons."

All the societies enlisted under the banner of charity organization supported this program, at least in theory, but each society was free to carry out its program in whatever way was best suited to local conditions. Where to begin, what activities to undertake were determined by the individual situation as long as the basic principles of the new charity were adhered to. Some of the guiding principles were: "There can be no personal charity without reverence for human nature as such." [23] "The true gift of charitable workers is the free bestowal of the time, patience and labor for finding out the right thing to do and the friendly sympathy which puts new heart into the despairing." [24] "The best service you can render to anyone needing aid is to help him help himself." [25] "Each person who falls out by the way has a personal history, is ignorant, is unfortunate, has had special reason for his present condition," [26] and in order to help him it was necessary to find out and, if possible, remove the cause of his trouble. The societies believed that each case was to be judged on its own merits. They also believed that relief should be adequate so as to enable the applicant to earn a sufficient living and be independent for the future.

With only these and a few other principles to serve them as guides, a few paid workers and many volunteers, most of them with little if any preparation, took over cheerfully and dauntlessly the responsibility for developing and carrying out these potentially unlimited programs. Charity organization was not for the fainthearted; it demanded of its disciples a keen intelligence, infinite patience, and a high degree of devotion.

14

References

1. Charles S. Loch, *Charity Organisation,* Swan Sonnenschein and Co., London, 1890.
2. S. Humphreys Gurteen, *A Handbook of Charity Organization,* published by the author, Buffalo, 1882, p. 132.
3. Sir Baldwin Leighton (ed.), *Letters and Other Writings of the Late Edward Denison,* Richard Bentley and Son, London, 1875, p. 80.
4. Octavia Hill, *Homes of the London Poor,* Macmillan and Co., London, 1875, p. 160.
5. Gurteen, *op. cit.,* pp. 38 and 39.
6. T. Guilford Smith, "The Best Development of the Central Work of a Society for Organizing Charity," *Proceedings of the National Conference of Charities and Correction: 1881,* p. 192.
7. Oscar C. McCulloch, "Associated Charities": Report of Committee on Charitable Organization in Cities, *Proceedings, NCCC: 1880,* p. 127.
8. Kathleen O'Meara, *Frederic Ozanam, His Life and Works,* Catholic School Book Co., New York, 1878, p. 61.
9. Margaret E. Rich, "The Modern Spirit of Earlier Days," *The Family,* Vol. IV, No. 9 (1924), p. 216.
10. Charles D. Kellogg, chairman, "Charity Organization in the United States": Report of the Committee on History of Charity Organization, *Proceedings, NCCC: 1893,* pp. 52–93.
11. *Ibid.*
12. D. O. Kellogg, "History of St. Matthew's Church, Francisville, Philadelphia, 1822–1925" (from a mimeographed statement of the Family Service Society of Philadelphia).
13. *Proceedings, NCCC: 1883,* pp. 88–89.
14. Margaret E. Rich, *Josephine Shaw Lowell,* Community Service Society of New York, New York, 1954.
15. Charles S. Fairchild, discussion, "Organization of Charities in Cities," *Proceedings, NCCC: 1883,* p. 126.
16. Oscar C. McCulloch, chairman, "The Organization of Charities": Report of the Standing Committee, *Proceedings, NCCC: 1889,* p. 13.
17. Charles D. Kellogg, *op. cit.,* p. 81.
18. J. W. Bachman, Report on Associated Charities of Chattanooga, *Proceedings, NCCC: 1883,* p. 139.
19. Alexander Johnson, "Oscar Carlton McCulloch," *The Family,* Vol. IV, No. 4 (1923), p. 80.
20. Josephine Shaw Lowell, "How to Adapt 'Charity Organization' Methods to Small Communities," *Proceedings, NCCC: 1887,* p. 135.
21. *Ibid.,* p. 136.
22. William Rhinelander Stewart, *The Philanthropic Work of Josephine Shaw Lowell,* Macmillan Co., New York, 1911, pp. 129–130.
23. Oscar C. McCulloch, "The Personal Element in Charity," *Proceedings, NCCC: 1885,* p. 343.
24. M. W. Moggridge, *Method in Almsgiving: A Handbook for Helpers,* John Murray, London, 1882.
25. *Hand-book for Friendly Visitors Among the Poor,* compiled and arranged by Charity Organization Society of the City of New York, G. P. Putnam's Sons, New York, 1883.
26. Oscar C. McCulloch, "The Personal Element in Charity" (*supra*).

II. Growth

BECAUSE OF THE time and thought usually given to exploring local needs and ways of meeting them before a charity organization society was actually launched, it was often possible, once it was organized, to move ahead with considerable speed. The New York City society, for example, by the end of the first year had set up six district offices, each with a paid agent and a district committee, and had enlisted 167 friendly visitors. It had a flourishing registration bureau in which 150 charitable agencies, including 88 churches, had listed 39,617 cases; a library containing 160 volumes and 1,000 pamphlets; and had published a manual for visitors and a directory of the charitable agencies of the city. The society also had several committees working on special projects—studies of legal relief, relief through loans, employment opportunities in the country as a whole, and the desirability of a woodyard as a labor test. The Boston society took over from its two sponsoring agencies a well-organized registration bureau and a group of friendly visitors along with the beginnings of district committees and some staff. In Boston, also, the publication of a directory of charities was undertaken in the society's first year.

Co-ordinating Efforts

The need to bring some kind of order out of the chaos of charitable giving was urgent not only in New York and Boston but in almost every community, whatever its size, and had to be approached from a number of different angles. Registration—the central listing of the names of relief recipients—was readily accepted in Boston and New York, though not in the beginning by all societies, as one means of bringing about co-operation and organized division of labor among charitable agencies. In Boston particularly the idea of co-operation through registration had received strong support. A commission consisting of George S. Hale, Alvah A. Burrage, and Augustus Parker reported on the subject in 1878 in a study of "The Treatment of the Poor": "Pauperism is more expensive than any judicious means for its prevention can be. . . . Some systematic plan for effective, full, and regular communication and co-operation between the public and private charities of the city and among the latter seems to us of the utmost importance." Registration was also expected to focus responsibility and act as a deterrent to careless, haphazard almsgiving. Zilpha D. Smith, first general secretary of the Boston Associated Charities, later commented, "Very few persons and fewer agencies had any idea of undertaking all round responsibility for any family. The exchange of information was one of the most important means of creating the sense of social responsibility." [1]

When a registration bureau was undertaken, it was usually located in the central office of the charity organization society. It offered agencies, churches, and individuals a place where they could list the names of those to whom they were giving alms, the amount given, and some information about the social status and character of the recipients. The lists of names were carefully safeguarded; the drawers containing them were locked and not even a board member had access to them. Eventually the bureaus became mere card catalogs with names, addresses, and identifying data about each applicant, and no other information except the name of the registering agency.

From the beginning, however, the intent of registration went far beyond a listing of relief recipients. Frances R. Morse, who was largely instrumental in starting the bureau in Boston, pointed out that it implied "not only the recording of information on charitable matters, but also the constant exchange of such information between societies and individuals engaged in charitable work. . . . The first good result expected from registration . . . was a wiser, more efficient, and helpful administration of relief, both public and private." The detection of imposture, which was often over-emphasized by the public, "fell into the second place and is not even mentioned in the first Boston circular." [2] Charles D. Kellogg, general secretary of the New York society, explained that "The apparatus was designed in pity and solicitude, not for the public, but for the miserable," [3] and Robert Treat Paine, president of the Boston Associated Charities, stated in the agency's first annual report that the main object was to see that relief was adapted to real needs: "It should make relief more full and prompt and tender. . . . Each one of the 7,716 cases reported is a human family, with human lives and cares and woes."

A registration bureau offered a way to make sure that, if relief grants came from different sources, they added up to an adequate sum and promoted the same objective. Miss Morse said, in the address from which we have quoted above, that registration was also expected to provide "authoritative information regarding the objects and resources of the various benevolent societies" to help in ascertaining whether existing agencies were adequate to meet existing needs; and through its street index, to construct a "map of social conditions. . . . We see that through certain houses and sometimes through certain streets moves a sad procession of people on the verge of pauperism—drinking, thriftless, thoughtless, half-sick—which is more often the cause of other conditions than is sometimes acknowledged." Registration was, indeed, an element of order and organization "but, if thoughtfully used, it is by no means only an element of order but becomes a strong incentive to personal service on behalf of those of our fellow citizens who, for one or another reason, are at a disadvantage." [4]

Not all registration bureaus lived up to these high expectations but they did gradually help to promote acquaintance and confidence among the agencies and to protect the individual family from unnecessary investigation and too much and too divergent

18

advice. Many of the "charities" and churches were slow to use the registration bureau and its sponsors had to interpret and demonstrate its value over and over again. In some instances a bureau undertook to copy the registration data from the records of reluctant agencies or "poor" officials. Many agencies undoubtedly resisted registration because it seemed to put the charity organization society in a position of superiority. An early writer on American charity stated: ". . . efficient co-operation in this matter on the part of all relieving agencies has been one of the most difficult results to secure. In some cities it has dwindled to almost nothing, in others it is very complete." [5] As late as 1888 it was reported at the National Conference that only 14 out of 35 charity organization societies had a registration bureau.[6] Eventually registration demonstrated its usefulness not only to relief agencies but to other agencies as well. With many changes in its methods and operation, the idea of registration is today embodied in a social service exchange or central index, usually operated by a council of social agencies.

Implicit in the idea of registration was the need for keeping records of help given and to whom, hitherto almost nonexistent. All the records, even those of the charity organization societies, were extremely meager but they did give some indication as to the number of relief recipients and usually some information as to whether they were widows with children, single men, or families where the breadwinner was sick or had deserted. From the data in the records and in the registration bureau, it was possible to get a rough picture of conditions in a given community—if not of the amount of poverty, at least of the amount of relief and the number and types of relief recipients. Comparison of the figures from different communities, even though likely to be incomplete, gave some factual basis for measuring increase or decrease of distress.

The printed word played a prominent part in the dissemination of information about the purpose of the new movement and did much to promote understanding and co-operation. Directories of charities, with classified lists of public and private agencies and descriptions of their work, antedated charity organization but the new societies quickly adopted this service because, as Zilpha Smith said:

> Local charities cannot co-operate unless they know of each other's existence and methods and such knowledge is generally wanting in the great cities. . . . The gathering of this information discovers unknown charities and reveals the gaps. To see that these gaps are filled by individual benevolence, by legislation, by extension of old organizations or the establishment of new, has been part of the work of organizing charity. Action of this sort has sometimes grown out of conferences of the various charities called by the societies for organizing charity.[7]

Annual reports and periodicals of various types, ranging from simple news bulletins to journals of considerable scope, were of help in developing lines of communication on charitable matters within individual communities and between communities. (More information on publications will be found in later chapters.)

In the larger cities the district offices of the charity organization society, in addition to their other functions, served as neighborhood information centers. The "district agent" was expected to have a thorough acquaintance with all the charities and churches in the area and to know the people who were receiving relief. From a report of the Committee on Charity Organization of the National Conference of Charities and Correction in 1883, we learn that the district committee, which usually met once a week, was open to representatives of agencies and churches and to interested individuals resident in the district "for mutual acquaintance, for exchange of information, for co-operation, for division of labor, for co-ordination of effort." [8]

Whether or not these meetings fulfilled the hope that they would create a unity of aims and methods in those who attended, they did bring about better inter-agency understanding and in some instances fostered a spirit of team play that was sadly needed. The board or council of a society also undertook to further such co-operation but the district committee had definite advantages: it met more frequently than the board, it was less formal, its focus was on individual situations, and all members could take part in discussion. In 1901 Mary E. Richmond pointed out that no machinery, however good, could be effective unless every board and staff member realized that co-operation must be a "working principle applicable to every act," that "charitable co-operation begins and ends in an intimate knowledge of the needs of individual poor people and in the patient endeavor to make them permanently better off." [9]

Principles of Investigation

Along with these efforts to promote co-ordination and co-operation, the charity organization societies were demonstrating what was meant by giving help in a discriminating way. Josephine Shaw Lowell, in an address printed in the *New York Evening Post,* February 20, 1897, expressed it thus: "We believe in discrimination, in treating each one of the unhappy men and women so far as it is possible as individuals, finding out about them and using the knowledge gained to do what is best for him or her."

To get this knowledge called for a careful investigation of each request for aid. Relief agencies also investigated applications for help but the new charity brought to the process a difference peculiarly its own. The manual of the New York Charity Organization Society (1883) explains:

> The surface-investigation which suffices for the Relief Visitor who is simply concerned with the fact of destitution and the question of temporary alleviation, will not satisfy the requirements of the more radical and permanent treatment which this Society aims to give. Our inquiries relate to *character* and antecedents, as well as circumstances, and must go far deeper, and need far more discrimination and study.[10]

And Octavia Hill, in a paper read before the Social Science Association of England in 1869, said:

> By knowledge of character more is meant than whether a man is a drunkard or a woman is dishonest; it means knowledge of the passions, hopes, and histories of people; where the temptation will touch them, what is the little scheme they made of their own lives, or would make, if they had encouragement; what training long-past phases of their lives may have afforded; how to move, touch, teach them. Our memories and our hopes are more truly factors of our lives than we often remember.[11]

Charity organization tried to make it clear that the purpose of investigation of applicants was not to find them out but to find out how to help them. To quote Robert Treat Paine again:

> The problem is, not *Is* he helpable? but *How* is he helpable? And when ingenuity is brought to bear, some way must be found. Years ago organized charity accepted the division into the worthy and the unworthy. Now we have exploded that as false and cruel, because

21

those who are unworthy are those who need some sort of help supremely.[12]

Investigation was essential if charity was to be a science, if it was to base what it did on facts; it was thought of as analogous to the diagnosis of the physician. This idea was expressed in 1893 by Daniel C. Gilman, president of Johns Hopkins University: "In social as in bodily ailments the art of healing must be based upon ascertained facts and on accumulated experience."[13] Many others had the same thought, among them Edward T. Devine, secretary of the New York society, who wrote: "It [investigation] is analogous to the diagnosis of the physician, who does not attempt to treat a serious malady from a glance at its superficial indications, but who carefully inquires into hidden and early manifestations of the disease, and seeks to know as much as possible of the complicating influences with which he must reckon in effecting a cure."[14]

Investigation, then, was not to protect the giver but to protect the recipient from ill-considered, perhaps harmful, aid not suited to his need. The relief agencies had felt an obligation to relieve only the worthy but charity organization societies moved beyond this concept and considered it essential to "protect this weak one, to restore this vicious one, [to put] on his feet again him who has fallen out by the way."[15] The purpose of investigation was to discover the need of the particular individual, to find out, as Dr. Devine wrote, "Are these applicants of ours ready to work out with us their own regeneration?"[16] One principle of charity organization was that the worker must tell the applicant that there was going to be an investigation and must explain the reasons for it. The investigation had value only if it was related to the good of the client; to use it as an end in itself was bad. In contrast to those who viewed investigation as a device for affixing a label, charity organizationists saw it as a prelude to providing adequate care. Mrs. Lowell wrote, in 1898, in the magazine *Charities,* "The only excuse for trespassing upon the privacy of other human beings . . . is that the person in distress has asked you to help him and that you cannot help him unless you know all about him." Unhappily, the general public continued for many years to think of investigation as synonymous with detection, partly perhaps as the result of earlier practice in relief giving and partly because what the new

22

societies did was not always in conformity with charity organization principles. The failure on the part of both the workers in the
societies and the general public to understand the principles and
method of investigation was the cause of much of the criticism,
often justified, of charity organization and its "red tape."

Some help might be provided before or during investigation but
as a rule investigation was expected to uncover the ills and suggest
a remedy: work for those able to do it, medical care for the sick,
economic help, preferably as a loan or obtained from some source
close to the person needing it. As late as 1893, something over 50
per cent of the charity organization societies did not give relief
from their own funds but raised it or "organized" it, case by case.
There were a number of reasons for this practice: the multiplicity
of relief agencies; a feeling that, in Mrs. Lowell's words, "relief
giving was an unnatural way of remedying the evils" of poverty;
and, most important of all, a fear that if money were available
workers would find it easier to give the money than to undertake
the more difficult tasks that would lead to the client's restoration.
It was feared they would lose sight of their real purpose of helping
the individual to develop his own neglected capabilities, thus
enabling him to be independent of charity for the future. As an
English writer put it, "It takes much more trouble to advise than to
give . . . the hasty half-crown." [17]

Some persons, including Zilpha Smith, were able to see that the
question of whether a society for organizing charity should give
relief "should not be confounded with that other question: Shall
relief be given?" She added, "There is not a charity organization
society in the country that does not believe that there are many
cases in which relief should be given." [18] Or, as the executive of
the London society expressed it, "We believe in charity, and in relief
as its mere instrument—in itself but little. We believe in the art
of charity." [19]

First Steps in Social Reform

Investigation of individual need, and attempts to meet it quickly,
confirmed the charity organization idea of what must be done if
"the poor" were to be permanently helped, if poverty was to be not
only cured but prevented. In the report of the first Committee on

the Organization of Charities in Cities, appointed by the National Conference in 1879, the chairman, Oscar McCulloch of Indianapolis, declared:

> There must be a change in some of the social conditions which press heavily upon them. Through already existing agencies, or new ones which spring up as the need of them is seen, the means of emergence from the ill conditions are offered. . . . And especially in the way of social reform can such a society exercise its greatest influence. It can insist on open spaces in the city for the recreation of the poor as Miss [Octavia] Hill has done. It can insist on the provision of better tenements for the poor both by calling public attention to their condition and by legal enactment. . . . There is no limit to its work or its power since in its idea it comprehends the association of all orders of talent, skill, and influence.[20]

What each society undertook to do in this broad area was determined by what it uncovered in the way of lacks and ill conditions in its day-by-day work. The society in Newport (Rhode Island), where employment was high in summer and low in winter, was organized in 1879 and in that same year started a penny savings fund with "deposits gathered by visitors, who call at houses for them . . . an ingenious system, which combines with great effectiveness the work of the Friendly Visitor with the encouragement of savings."[21] By 1893 seventeen other societies had set up similar though not identical savings schemes. Another device was a fuel or coal fund, which visitors collected in the summer to pay for the winter coal.

In 1880 the Buffalo society started the Fitch Creche, a day nursery for the children of employed mothers and later an employment bureau to help the mothers find work. By 1893 twenty-two societies had either started or persuaded other groups to start day nurseries or kindergartens. Other projects designed to lead to self-help included a variety of opportunities for training—laundries, cooking schools, supervised sewing rooms, schools for domestics, and so on. In the New Haven society, mothers' meetings were held for instruction in making and mending clothes. Poughkeepsie had kitchen gardens and the agency in Portland (Maine) ran a workroom for women. Woodyards provided a work test for able-bodied men and gave them a chance to earn some emergency relief, although it was clearly recognized that relief earned by work was still relief.

24

At the National Conference in 1897 a report was made on some experiments by societies in running employment bureaus. It was the experience of most of them that it was not wise to act as an employment office except in dealing with individuals after investigation. In Brooklyn, requests from employers soon exceeded the power of the bureau to supply workers from families in need of assistance, and applications for work from those not in need of assistance occupied a large proportion of the time of the agents of the society. "To permit such a condition to continue and to grow would interfere seriously with the business of the regular employment bureaus and intelligence offices of the city." Moreover, there were doubts as to the desirability of any free employment bureau: "It is bad for anyone to get something for nothing, if it is possible for him to earn it. A free employment bureau may have a pauperizing and demoralizing influence as truly as a free soup-house. . . . The charity organization society [could be] chiefly useful in finding work for the people who fall between classes, where the good work of a friend or the ingenuity of a visitor is needed." [22]

Stimulating New Social Enterprises

There was always the danger that a society eager to prove its value might take on so many activities that it would be able to do none of them well and might break of its own weight and lack of cohesion. "The position of the society, as a helper, not a rival, is more clearly seen, if it keeps its hands free from such extra work." [23] For this reason it was thought preferable to stimulate others to develop needed agencies, to confine charity organization efforts to the demonstration of a service that might later be taken over by another group, or to contribute to other groups what it had learned about ways of helping.

Thus, the Lynn (Massachusetts) society carried on an active program of child welfare; on the other hand, the Philadelphia society promoted the reorganization of a separate agency for the care of children. In both of these projects, as in other children's services, charity organization principles and methods were adopted and adapted to meet the needs of children. The value of charity organization methods was also demonstrated in another field—that of providing care for the victims of disaster. A flood in Cincinnati in 1884, a serious fire that occurred in Lynn in 1888, and a tornado in Louisville in 1890 called for rapid mobilization of resources and orderly distribution of relief. In each instance the local charity organization society assumed leadership and developed procedures that subsequently proved useful in other disaster relief programs. The San Francisco agency was one of the first to work out a plan for charities endorsement in co-operation with the chamber of commerce.

Hospitals drew upon charity organization societies for help in determining the eligibility of patients for free medical care. The London Charity Organisation Society saw a further need and in 1895 worked out a plan to place social workers as "almoners" in a few hospitals to assist patients in the effective use of medical care, the society paying half the salary. Ten years later the Massachusetts General Hospital in Boston established a hospital social service department, the first in the United States, adapting charity organization methods to meet the social problems of the sick.

Frequently the initiation of a special enterprise came not from a society or its board but from individual board members or volunteers. Robert Treat Paine, president of the Boston Associated Charities from 1879 to 1907, was responsible for starting in that city a remedial loan association to conduct a loan business free of the abuses common to most such businesses at that time. In Baltimore the Rev. Maltbie Babcock learned from parishioners who were active in the Charity Organization Society about families' paying ruinous interest on loans. After correspondence with Mr. Paine in Boston and consultation with Miss Richmond, Dr. Babcock prevailed on the businessmen of his acquaintance to organize a loan business operating on an equitable basis. In 1894 the New York Charity Organization Society sponsored a similar undertaking, which soon became an independent enterprise under the name of the Provident Loan Association. Under the Baltimore society's leadership a national remedial loan association was organized in 1908.

Indeed, the interests of most board members were not limited to the activities of the societies they represented. Mr. Paine also established Wells Memorial, a non-sectarian center for artisans and mechanics. It was managed by a committee of workingmen and

26

its halls were open as meeting places for trade unions, which had frequently been obliged to meet in rooms over saloons. Mrs. Josephine Shaw Lowell, of the New York society, gave time and thought to many enterprises involving the care of those who were ill or distressed and to activities for the improvement of working conditions and wages. Among these was the Working Women's Society out of which grew the Consumers' League in New York City and later similar leagues in other cities and the National Consumers' League. Oscar McCulloch, the pastor of a large and popular church, not only helped organize the Indianapolis Charity Organization Society but later took a major part in the movement for a State Board of Charities in Indiana and served as one of its members. Robert W. deForest, president of the New York Charity Organization Society from 1888 until his death in 1931, worked for a number of legislative reforms notably in connection with housing, accepted political appointment when it furthered the causes charity organization stood for, joined the fight against child labor, and was recognized as a leader in social thought, nationally as well as locally.

Important as it was to make sure that community resources were adequate to cure distress, it was even more important to discover and root out the conditions that caused the distress. The Buffalo society had an early opportunity to demonstrate how scientific charity could accomplish this aim. Gurteen described the situation and the action taken by the society:

> The grain shovellers, who worked in the holds of vessels, shovelling grain to the leg of the elevators, lived, during working hours, in an atmosphere of intense heat and thick dust, which, on an average, produced death by "elevator pneumonia" within five years. . . . The wages were high, but the work lasted only for a few months; and at the end of the season . . . the men were left penniless, and in a weakened condition, to get a living as best they could. The natural consequence was that each winter a large number . . . became dependent upon public and private charity, while others died . . . leaving wife and children to be supported by the city. Few, beyond the business men actually engaged in the grain trade, knew anything of this crying evil, and had it not been for the action of the Charity Organization Society [to which the families of the shovellers became known], no reform would have been attempted.[24]

The society gathered the facts, enlisted the co-operation of other agencies, and through united action—"band work," as Gurteen

27

called it—and organization the city was persuaded to pass an ordinance correcting these "ill conditions of work."

The "Retail Method" of Social Reform

This "retail method" of social reform was a characteristic feature of charity organization societies. From the plight of one individual or family they undertook, as Zilpha Smith said, "to distinguish between what is peculiar to that family and must be individually conquered and what is borne in common with all its little community and must be cured by social or legislative action." [25] They collected the factual evidence, usually through the contacts of agents and volunteers, sometimes by special studies, interpreted its significance in terms of human suffering and misery, and organized a concerted attack upon legislators and other officials.

In Chattanooga, for instance, the society, which was organized in 1881, in the next year, according to one of its board members, the Rev. J. W. Bachman, "prepared three bills, one for a Reform School for Boys and Girls, one for a Hospital, and one for a State Board of Charity, and put them before the legislature. They passed the second reading but never finally got through, but we hope at the next meeting of the legislature we will get them through." [26]

In 1882 the Boston Associated Charities appointed a Committee on Dwellings of the Poor to investigate and attempt to improve housing conditions. "How small a tenement," asked the president of the society, "how little light and air in a dwelling shall this community tolerate? Let us sweep out of existence everything below that minimum." [27] Housing had been recognized as a problem by earlier charitable agencies, as was noted in Chapter I, and in most of the larger cities the charity organization societies worked steadfastly and patiently over the years to bring about improvement—to establish standards and to obtain legislation that would ensure decent living conditions. Thus the New York Charity Organization Society joined forces with the Buffalo society in getting the state legislature to pass a tenement house bill and played an active part in ensuring its enforcement.

The effect of poor housing and overcrowding on health had been proved repeatedly. One study in New York City had shown the high incidence of tuberculosis in a tenement house notorious for its lack of light and air, and for its poor sanitation and insufficient space. The New York Charity Organization Society, along with its work for tenement house reform, inaugurated a committee on the prevention of tuberculosis, with representatives of medical and other interested groups. The work of this committee led to similar plans in other cities, under other auspices, and contributed to the later organization of the National Association for the Study and Prevention of Tuberculosis. It was common practice for the charity organization agency to concern itself with the problems facing the local board of health, such as the safeguarding of the milk and water supply, providing adequate hospital facilities (especially for patients with contagious diseases), and securing competent supervision of municipal hospitals. Many societies either started a visiting nurse association or were instrumental in getting some other local group to start one.

The various efforts of the societies to do away with begging and vagrancy—"to extirpate mendicancy" as it was phrased in many constitutions—were untiring but discouraging in results, primarily because it was and still is a national as well as a local problem and called for the kind of control that was impossible for a non-governmental agency to exercise. In New York City and Philadelphia special officers were employed to suppress street begging. In some cities the arrest of street beggars was effective to some degree, but the agencies felt the best means of solving the problem was to educate the public to refrain from indiscriminate giving—a job that had to be carried on continuously.

The drifter, who had no legal residence, was a more serious problem than the person who had some claim of belonging in a given community. Tramps often were lodged in the police station or given a train ticket to the next city or to another state. The charity organization societies viewed these procedures as inhumane, dangerous from the point of view of health, and unlikely to cure or to prevent the habit of vagrancy. Many societies started wayfarers' lodges as one of their first projects or persuaded the municipality to provide a lodging house where men could have bed and meals in return for a specified amount of wood-chopping or other work. Another approach was to procure legislation authorizing the commitment of able-bodied vagrants to a house of correction.

29

As one way of curbing the practice of getting rid of the wanderer by passing him on to another community whether or not he requested it, the Committee on Charity Organization of the National Conference of Charities and Correction formulated a charitable Transportation Agreement based on one in use among the Jewish agencies. Under this agreement, which all charitable agencies both public and private were urged to observe, the most important provision was that transportation should be given only when the giver had made sure that the traveler's situation would be improved in the town to which he was being sent. Charity organization societies not only signed the agreement themselves but undertook to spread its gospel among other agencies. The Transportation Agreement was not a solution of the problem of vagrancy but its supporters were able to prove that it prevented much aimless drifting and frequently helped the runaway boy or girl, the ill or out-of-work person, to reach a place where he could be cared for.

Typical of the movements stimulated or carried on by charity organization agencies in different cities, based always on needs revealed in the care of individuals or families, were the following: industrial training for the young, school attendance laws, child labor legislation, facilities for legal advice for those unable to pay, improvement in labor conditions and wages, prevention of industrial accidents, promotion of juvenile courts and probation, legislation on wife desertion and non-support, better care for the mentally retarded, and workmen's compensation laws. Francis H. McLean, who was field secretary of the Field Department of *Charities and The Commons,* said in 1908, "The reforms which have been attempted—and charity organization societies have been mixed up in many kinds of reforms—have all grown out of more and more careful case work."

The responsibility of the societies did not end when their objective was realized; it was necessary to guard against lowering of standards or failure to carry out the intent of any new provisions. Nor did they neglect other aspects of the more abundant life that "scientific charity" was pledged to bring about. Zilpha Smith wrote in the Boston publication, *Lend a Hand,* "A human soul needs more than work, good as work is, and some provision must be made for pleasures, for an occasional hour of freedom and for society." Joseph Lee, who was later to become active in the National Recreation Association, was, in his early years, a friendly visitor for the Boston Associated Charities and was deeply impressed with the society's campaign for the first playground in Boston. In a letter to the *Boston Transcript* in 1926 he wrote:

> She [Zilpha Smith] first made a little map of Boston, with all the open spaces marked, back somewhere about 1890, had a study made of the districts that were most congested and most needed open spaces. The two places where the need was proved to be the greatest were the South Bay district and the North End. The big Randolph Street Playground in the former and the recent development in the latter were— the former directly and the latter indirectly—concrete results [of her campaign].

Josephine Shaw Lowell of the New York Charity Organization Society was similarly concerned about the lack of wholesome outlets for the "natural energy of boys and girls" and played an active part in establishing playgrounds. In Baltimore, as well as in other cities, the society was successful in promoting concerts which would provide good music at low cost. The role of charity organization in these and other ventures was primarily to show a need, to organize community support, and then to induce other groups to sponsor the enterprise. In most cities the societies were for many years "the inspirers, directors and organizers of the philanthropic work of the entire community . . . giving individual service and fostering co-operation." [28]

The Friendly Visitor

None of these objectives—community co-operation, the restoration of individuals and families in distress, and the prevention of misery through the changing of community conditions—could be attained "except by sincere and devoted personal effort on the part of at least a few individuals." [29] The charity organization idea of providing for each troubled individual or family a friendly visitor who would give sympathetic counsel and rekindle hope and self-respect, of bringing together those who could give and those who had need of the gifts of friendship, had been tried at various times in many countries. The pattern developed in the United States owed something to all of these experiments but most to the in-

31

fluence and teachings of Octavia Hill, who, in her work with her tenants in London, had demonstrated that if the poor were to be raised to a permanently better condition they had to be dealt with as individuals by individuals, and for this work volunteers had to be found, to serve as friendly visitors.

The specific meaning of the term "friendly visitor" was explained by Zilpha Smith:

> There is a great deal of visiting which is friendly which we do not include in our definition of "friendly visiting." The district nurses, kindergartners and savings collectors visit among the poor; but their interest is chiefly on one side of their life, and may be dropped at any time. The friendly visitor visits very few families . . . but her intercourse with them is on many sides. . . . The friendly visitor is associated with the family, and not with a district.[30]

In the teachings of Octavia Hill, as given in her writings, there was no place for sentimentality or patronage; the visitor would gain as much as she gave because the "poor *have* lessons to teach us of patience, vigor, and content." Almsgiving by the visitor was forbidden because it would destroy the possibility of really good relations with the family—"Rich and poor should know one another simply and naturally as friends." Miss Hill stressed the need for organizing the visitors, for training and oversight and advice along the way so that their efforts might be strengthened and directed and inevitable periods of discouragement overcome. The preliminary investigation was to be made by the paid agent; the volunteer visitor would give the personal service "to develop the resources of the poor themselves." * The friendly visitors went into the homes, bringing what Charles D. Kellogg called the "alms of understanding, prudence, discretion, counsel, friendship."[31]

In thus offering a channel for disciplined and systematized volunteer service, charity organization undertook to organize not only the charities of the community but its charitable impulses as well. Jeffrey R. Brackett, writing in 1903, said: "The aim of the societies is not to be a mechanism for doing charity for others but to be a

---

* The charity organization leaders in London called this personal service "case work," a term not used in the United States until probably 1897. See M. W. Moggridge, *Method in Almsgiving: A Handbook for Helpers*, London, 1882, p. 89; also Charles S. Loch, *Charity Organisation*, Swan Sonnenschein & Co., London, 1890, p. 51.

means of developing the resources of individual givers and doers." [32] Twenty years earlier Mrs. James T. Fields quoted Joseph Tuckerman in a pamphlet published by the Boston Associated Charities: "Only by creating a feeling of relationship and connection between different classes of society can we ever bring about any great and permanent amelioration of the condition of the poor, any great and permanent means for the prevention of pauperism and crime."

Paid workers, of varying backgrounds and abilities, were in the minority. There was usually one as executive and, in districted societies, one in each district. The societies had been started by volunteers as had the earlier relief agencies. Individuals like Frances Morse and Mrs. James T. Fields in Boston, Josephine Shaw Lowell in New York, John Glenn in Baltimore, Oscar McCulloch in Indianapolis, and a host of others not only helped to plan and interpret the need for a charity organization society but raised money and did the actual work necessary to get the agency launched. Most of these pioneer leaders continued to give generously of their time and energy as long as they lived. They served on boards and committees and helped the paid workers learn their jobs. They served as friendly visitors, as did all members of board and staff, and they enlisted and trained other volunteers.

The idea of a friendly visitor—"a visiting friend"—for every family, with no visitor to have more than two or three families, literally called for hundreds of devoted men and women. It represented a great experiment in citizen participation, in applied democracy. It was universally accepted as a principle of charity organization but its application in practice fell far short of what had been hoped for. Where it was most successful—in Boston, Baltimore, Philadelphia, Chicago, Cincinnati, and a few other cities —valiant, patient work gave to many distressed families the encouragement and help they needed.

Theoretically, there was a clear distinction between the responsibilities of the paid worker or "agent" and those of the friendly visitor. Zilpha Smith explained that both paid agents and volunteers were needed—"the paid worker to make the first inquiries and help the [district] committee to direct the visitors; the volunteers to bring to the agent and to each other the resources of their varied lives and to give to the two or three poor families each makes his

33

friends that constant personal sympathy and interest which it is impossible for any agent to give to the hundreds of families he knows." [33]

This differentiation was not always adhered to consistently, partly because friendly visitors tended, as the years passed, to feel that the paid worker could do the work better than a volunteer, and partly because the ideal of a friend for every family was never fully realized, even in the cities where recruiting of friendly visitors was most successful. Even Boston, where the number of friendly visitors was larger than in other cities, found it a "perpetual struggle" to get and hold competent visitors. The work of friendly visiting had been started there before the organization of the Associated Charities. Robert Treat Paine said it was "promoted chiefly by two ladies . . . with a degree of fine enthusiasm that was really wonderful." [34]

This enthusiasm was infectious and led others to join the ranks. Another reason for Boston's 800 friendly visitors was the care taken in training them, the encouragement and patience that helped them over the hard spots. Zilpha Smith tells about this training:

> At the beginning, every new visitor is a care and a burden to the agent and [district] committee. Friendly visitors are not sought in order to lighten our work. We are not wishing to get rid of burdens by shifting them upon new shoulders. Friendly visitors are wanted because in the end their service makes for the good of the poor people, for the good of the whole community. [35]

The visitors themselves were often surprised at what they could accomplish if they, too, were patient. Mrs. Roger Wolcott, a Boston board member, gave an illustration:

> The friendly visitor, by tact and delicate suggestion, must instil a desire for cleanliness, so necessary to self-respect. Mr. William D. Howells, who during his recent residence in Boston gave much of his valuable time as a visitor for the Associated Charities, was amused one day to be told, on knocking at the door of a house where he had studiously endeavored to inspire a sense of cleanliness, that he could not come in, as the floor had just been washed and he might soil it again. [36]

In addition to their service to individual families the friendly visitors were able, out of their own experience, to interpret the new charity to the community and to give the support of enlightened public opinion to efforts for the improvement of conditions that were causing poverty and distress. Amos G. Warner makes this point clear:

> The influence of the visiting upon the poor may be excellent, but there can be no doubt that one of its very greatest benefits is upon the visitors. It is a method by which we may hope to reach "the upper classes.". . . . There is no education in charity work so good as that which comes to the friendly visitor. Becoming interested in one family, he is likely to be led out into an interest in all branches of city government and of the county and state government as well, and may even have his attention drawn to the need of federal prevention of undesirable immigration. He who takes an interest in trying to cure poverty in a single case will soon come to find that nothing in politics or industry is foreign to him.[37]

References

1. Zilpha D. Smith, in a letter to *The Family*, Vol. IV, No. 3 (1923), p. 76.
2. Frances R. Morse, "Registration of Charitable Relief," *Proceedings of International Congress of Charities, Correction, and Philanthropy: 1893* (Section on Charity Organization), Johns Hopkins Press, Baltimore, 1894, pp. 99, 102.
3. Charles D. Kellogg, "Statistics: Their Value in Charity Organization Work," *Proceedings of the National Conference of Charities and Correction: 1890,* p. 35.
4. Morse, *loc. cit.*
5. Amos G. Warner, *American Charities*, Thomas Y. Crowell & Co., New York, 1894, p. 382.
6. Zilpha D. Smith, chairman, "Organization of Charities": Report of the Committee on the Organization of Charity, *Proceedings, NCCC: 1888*, p. 125.
7. *Ibid.*
8. Report of the Standing Committee on the Organization of Charities in Cities, *Proceedings, NCCC: 1883*, pp. 72–73.
9. Mary E. Richmond, "Charitable Co-operation," *Proceedings, NCCC: 1901*, pp. 298, 313.
10. *Hand-book for Friendly Visitors Among the Poor*, compiled and arranged by Charity Organization Society of the City of New York, G. P. Putnam's Sons, New York, 1883, p. 6.
11. Octavia Hill, "Importance of Aiding the Poor Without Almsgiving," quoted by C. Edmund Maurice (ed.), *Life of Octavia Hill as Told in Her Letters*, Macmillan & Co., London, 1913, p. 258.
12. Robert Treat Paine, discussion on charity organization, *Proceedings, NCCC: 1899*, p. 355.
13. Daniel C. Gilman, "A Panorama of Charitable Work in Many Lands," *Proceedings of International Congress of Charities, Correction, and Philanthropy: 1893 (supra).*
14. Edward T. Devine, *The Practice of Charity*, Lentilhon & Co., New York, 1901, p. 45.

15. Oscar C. McCulloch, "The Personal Element in Charity," *Proceedings, NCCC: 1885*, p. 341.
16. Edward T. Devine, "The Values and the Dangers of Investigation," *Proceedings, NCCC: 1897*, p. 194.
17. M. W. Moggridge, *Method in Almsgiving: A Handbook for Helpers*, John Murray, London, 1882.
18. Zilpha D. Smith, discussion on charity organization, *Proceedings, NCCC: 1888*, p. 412.
19. Charles S. Loch, *Charity Organisation*, Swan Sonnenschein and Co., London, 1890, p. 105.
20. Oscar C. McCulloch, "Associated Charities": Report of Committee on Charitable Organization in Cities, *Proceedings, NCCC: 1880*, p. 134.
21. Charles D. Kellogg, chairman, "Charity Organization in the United States": Report of the Committee on History of Charity Organization, *Proceedings, NCCC: 1893*, p. 80.
22. Charles E. Bartram, "Free Public Employment Offices," *Proceedings, NCCC: 1897*, pp. 212–216.
23. Zilpha D. Smith, chairman, "Organization of Charities": Report of the Committee on the Organization of Charity, *Proceedings, NCCC: 1888*, p. 123.
24. S. Humphreys Gurteen, *A Handbook of Charity Organization*, published by the author, Buffalo, 1882, pp. 194–195. (Also referred to by McCulloch in his committee report of 1880.)
25. Zilpha D. Smith, "Needy Families in Their Homes: Introduction," *Proceedings, NCCC: 1901*, p. 287.
26. J. W. Bachman, Report on Associated Charities of Chattanooga, *Proceedings, NCCC: 1883*, pp. 139–140.
27. Margaret E. Rich, quoting Robert Treat Paine, in "The Modern Spirit of Earlier Days," *The Family*, Vol. IV, No. 9 (1924), p. 220.
28. Charles Richmond Henderson and others, *Modern Methods of Charity*, Macmillan Co., New York, 1904, p. 443.
29. Josephine Shaw Lowell, "How to Adapt 'Charity Organization' Methods to Small Communities," *Proceedings, NCCC: 1887*, p. 137.
30. Zilpha D. Smith, "Needy Families in Their Homes: Friendly Visiting," *Proceedings, NCCC: 1901*, p. 398.
31. Charles D. Kellogg, "Charity Organization as an Educating Force," *Proceedings, NCCC: 1892*, p. 451.
32. Jeffrey Richardson Brackett, *Supervision and Education in Charity*, Macmillan Co., New York, 1903, p. 148.
33. Zilpha D. Smith, chairman, "Organization of Charities": Report of the Committee on the Organization of Charity, *Proceedings, NCCC: 1888*, p. 127.
34. Robert Treat Paine, discussion, *Proceedings of International Congress of Charities, Correction, and Philanthropy: 1893 (supra)*, p. 17.
35. Zilpha D. Smith, discussion on friendly visiting, *Proceedings, NCCC: 1901*, p. 406.
36. Mrs. Roger Wolcott, "Friendly Visiting," *Proceedings of International Congress of Charities, Correction, and Philanthropy: 1893 (supra)*, p. 110.
37. Amos G. Warner, *American Charities*, Thomas Y. Crowell & Co., New York, 1894, pp. 390–391.

III. The Emergence of a Profession

ONE OF THE features of the new charity which set it off from the old was its insistence that its workers, both volunteer and paid, must be trained, that scientific charity called for knowledge and skill as well as good intentions. Octavia Hill, whose work in London had had a marked influence on the development of the charity organization movement in the United States, was among the first to see the need for training. In one of her "Essays," which were compiled and published by the Boston Associated Charities, she had proposed definite plans for advising and helping the inexperienced visitor and had suggested some points to be covered, adding that there were no general rules that would obviate the necessity of thought. As a beginning it was important for board and staff members to understand charity organization philosophy and principles and to learn all that experience had taught.

Pamphlets, books, and reprints were gathered from a variety of sources. A few manuals or guides for visitors were developed, some by the London Charity Organisation Society, some by societies in this country, which gave practical information about resources, about local laws and ordinances, and often something about marketing, cooking, and similar matters affecting family life. These guides suggested that visitors must have delicacy, tact, respect, and sympathy and urged them to get acquainted with all members of a family, to look at life from their point of view, not to act until they understood what was needed. Mrs. James J. Putnam of the Boston agency pointed out that visitors must bear in mind that "many of the evils cannot be cured except by persistent effort of the people themselves." The writers of the guides or manuals agreed with Octavia Hill that there were no rules and that visitors would have to develop resourcefulness, imagination, and ingenuity.

Much of this early training material was excellent and most societies started libraries almost as soon as they opened offices.* It soon became apparent, however, that much more precise methods were needed and that the societies themselves must take responsibility for formulating a systematized body of knowledge if a science of charity were to be developed. Robert Treat Paine, president of the Boston Associated Charities, suggested, in 1881, that the societies should lose no time in starting the search for such knowledge: "It seems to me a matter of the greatest importance that we should carefully study in what way we can best help towards a permanent restoration of families who seem to be going downward. I know of no greater and more valuable contribution that can be made to scientific charity than a practical treatise giving practical methods in their actual operation and with the results;—the methods by which poor families and struggling families in all their various phases can be really and permanently helped." [1] The treatise was not immediately forthcoming but the idea of careful

---

* These libraries usually included books by Octavia Hill, *The Life and Letters of Edward Denison,* Gurteen's *A Handbook of Charity Organization* (1882), the annual *Proceedings* of the National Conference of Charities and Correction, occasional papers of the London Charity Organisation Society, manuals and guides for visitors, annual reports of agencies, reprints of articles, and periodicals, such as the *Monthly Register* (started in 1879 by the Philadelphia Society for Organizing Charity).

The National Conference of Charities and Correction Committee on Charitable Organization in Cities gave a reading list in its first report (1880) which included: *Our Common Land, Homes of the London Poor,* and *Essays* (compiled and published by the Boston Associated Charities), all by Octavia Hill; *Phases of Charity* and *Provident Schemes* by Gurteen, London *Charity Organisation Reporter* (Weekly); *Monthly Register.*

In the Committee report for 1884 a few titles were added: Gurteen's *A Handbook of Charity Organization; How to Help the Poor* by Mrs. James T. Fields; *Wisdom in Charity* by C. G. Ames; *Importance of Uniting Individual and Associated Volunteer Effort in Behalf of the Poor* by Louisa Lee Schuyler; *Method in Almsgiving* by M. W. Moggridge; *Public Relief and Private Charity* by Josephine Shaw Lowell.

study of "practical methods in their actual operation" persisted and eventually such study, by many people in different places and at different times, laid the foundation for skilled service to families and individuals. In the meantime, it was necessary to train workers even though recorded experience was meager, no textbooks were yet written, and those responsible for training were themselves learning as they taught.

Early Training Courses

The First Annual Report of the New York Charity Organization Society, in 1883, tells of "training workers for new districts when they shall be formed." The method and content of the training are not given but we note that regular meetings were held for "the promotion of unity of action and methods." The Committee on District Work had weekly discussions of "case reports" under the leadership of Josephine Shaw Lowell, who was a staunch supporter of scientific charity. Later Mrs. Lowell held meetings of district "agents" (the term used for paid workers for many years), as a "means of giving training to the inexperienced and counsel and encouragement to those who had been longer at work."

The district or case committee was another instrument for training. At the meetings of these committees, usually held once a week, volunteers and paid staff discussed the situations of individual applicants. Through these discussions, as Oscar McCulloch expressed it, "the nebulous mass of 'the poor' resolves itself into individual units each capable of pain and of pleasure." [2] There also the friendly visitors gave reports and exchanged ideas on what had proved successful or otherwise in their work with families. Many of these reports revealed practical application of charity organization principles and were often well in advance of the thinking of the time. One visitor, for instance, reported that in her experience, a drinking man would keep a pledge to stay sober for a day when he could not keep, even for a day, one that bound him for a year. In the Annual Report of the Boston Associated Charities in 1889, another visitor reported, in dealing with intemperance, that "something can be done toward improvement through watchfulness and the influence of the expected frequent call and personal presence of the visitor. But a cure can seldom be accomplished except by means not yet available, namely, the enforced commitment of the victim of alcoholic disease to an asylum devoted to the malady." Here were the practical procedures charity organization societies were looking for, but unfortunately there was no means of collecting them and making them available to the field as a whole.

Nearly all agencies accepted the idea of training as they accepted other charity organization principles, but what was actually taught varied greatly from agency to agency. In spite of these variations, by 1888 sufficient progress in training workers had been made to impel Amos G. Warner, the executive of the Baltimore Charity Organization Society, in a lecture given at Johns Hopkins University, to make an optimistic statement: "To some the term scientific charity seems a perversion of terms, an instance of confused thinking that results from a tendency to count our sciences before they are hatched. Yet something to which it can be applied is very palpably coming into existence."

In the same year, Zilpha D. Smith, reporting for the Committee on the Organization of Charity at the National Conference of Charities and Correction, summarized the current thinking on the points to be covered in the training of district agents:

> An agent for public relief has to learn whether there is destitution, if the family can be trusted to use relief well and such facts of residence and payment of taxes as determine whether a city or town or the commonwealth shall pay for the relief. The agent of a society for organizing charity has likewise to learn the need and the character of the family but also much more. If there is sickness he must learn from the physician its character and what, besides the physician's own care is needed to secure recovery. If members of the family might work he must learn what they know how to do and get the opinion of former employers. Relatives are to be sought out, old friends found again, the official record searched for the data for a pension or something else devised which shall discover the solution of the difficulty. . . . A London agent . . . confirmed the experiences of workers in this country, that to let a woman tell her own story in her own way gave a much better idea of her character than to draw it from her by set questions. . . . To talk with a poor person—a stranger—in such a way as to elicit at the first visit all the information necessary is a matter requiring skill and experience. The paid agent, giving every day to the work, gains this skill, and also a general acquaintance with the conditions of life in his district, which enables him to see the bearing of trifles which would escape a less constant worker and may prove clews to the real difficulty.[3]

40

Further advance in training came with the first systematized class for workers started by the Boston society in 1891. Workers-in-training, usually not more than five in any one year, were given practice under the supervision of experienced agents, attended discussion sessions led by the general secretary, and were assigned related reading. The supervising agents met periodically with the general secretary to discuss both content and method of training. Also in 1891 the Brooklyn society gave a well-planned and successful course for volunteers, meeting weekly over a twelve-week period.

These two ventures stimulated similar plans in other cities but the results left much to be desired. There was no fixed pattern for the courses and much of the so-called training was too general to be of value. Charles D. Kellogg, executive of the New York Charity Organization Society, in 1892 voiced the dissatisfaction felt by many of his colleagues:

> Any person or association which insists that our present methods are good enough is either very indifferent to the welfare of the poor or very conceited. Charity Organization insists on the reverse, imploring men and women to come together and search out what needs to be done. It invites conferences for the freest exchange of views by either critics or friends. It strives to establish communication between workers in all kinds of philanthropy. . . . The general cause of charity is advanced by the full and free comparison of methods and especially by deliberation over actual cases of an individual nature.[4]

The following year Mary E. Richmond, the new, young general secretary of the Baltimore Charity Organization Society, started a series of "educational conferences" for friendly visitors by the presentation of the history of the society's work with one family. In *The Charities Record,* published by that agency, she said, "The family selected was the most discouraging one we could find and it was hoped that the amount of work shown to have been done without any encouraging results would teach us all to profit by our own blunders and would point out some of the reasons for our failure." Deliberation over actual cases soon proved its value as a method of teaching and learning and was used not only in agency classes but later in more formal courses as well. The work recorded might be poor, the records themselves meager—as they usually were—but Miss Richmond believed that, if the reasons for blunders and failures could be discovered, the discussions might lead to improved work and possibly to improved recording. In 1896 Charles S. Loch,

41

general secretary of the London Charity Organisation Society, visited Baltimore. Miss Richmond later wrote that "it was during that visit that I saw for the first time a case record—one brought from England—which marched from definite premises toward a definite conclusion. . . . He made me see . . . that the constructive, purposeful mind was not behind our entries." [5]

As part of their avowed purpose to improve the quality of all work for those in distress, many of the charity organization societies opened their training classes to workers in other agencies. In this way they encouraged the application of charity organization principles and methods in other types of charitable work and gave their own workers a broader understanding of philanthropy in general. Agency training programs also benefited both directly and indirectly from the courses on charity organization and social problems in colleges, universities, and theological seminaries, courses which the charity organization societies had done much to encourage. By 1893 some dozen colleges and universities and about the same number of divinity schools had courses on charities and correction, applied ethics, or social sciences, and within the next ten years the number more than doubled.

The classroom work was usually supplemented by excursions to charitable and correctional institutions, and sometimes by volunteer service in an agency or by a piece of practical research. Professor Albert O. Wright, president of the National Conference in 1896, said, "Philanthropy is thus raised to the rank of a science, the practical and theoretical are yoked together, and a large number of able young men and women are looking forward to make this their life work." [6] In a few instances, heads of charitable or correctional agencies were invited to supplement the instruction of the regular faculty. The courses were of great value in stimulating a practical interest in social conditions and many of their graduates engaged in some type of philanthropic work or gave competent service as board members and volunteers in their home communities.

Launching a School of Philanthropy

In 1893 the possibility of a more ambitious approach to training for charitable work came from two different sources. The Women's

Settlement in Southwark, London, started a two-year course in "philanthropic training" with practice work divided between the Charity Organisation Society and the Settlement, and at the International Congress of Charities, Correction, and Philanthropy in Chicago, in 1893, Anna L. Dawes, a board member from Pittsfield, Massachusetts, urged that a training school for charity workers be established in this country. A little later the suggestion was strongly supported by Amos G. Warner, a teacher of the social sciences who had had experience in both public and private charities:

> The development of a new profession is manifestly underway. As yet preparation is obtained mainly through experience as doctors of medicine used to obtain their training by being in the office of an established practitioner; but this condition of things will be progressively modified in one line of practice as it has been in the other. . . . Training in the new profession will be important. . . . [It] should include both didactic instruction and practice under expert guidance.[7]

Dissatisfaction with agency training was expressed freely—it was too limited and it specialized too soon—but the proposed remedy of establishing some kind of school was slow in being accepted, or perhaps, following the usual charity organization procedure, the idea merely needed time to take root and grow. Certainly some thought was being given to the idea of a school, notably by Mary Richmond, who had greeted the London experiment with enthusiasm and who spoke strongly in favor of school training:

> Charity as a profession is still in its infancy, but here and there one finds even now the charity agent of exceptional ability with power to acquire an organized body of knowledge in a disorganized field. . . . These exceptional workers, underpaid and overworked, are the pioneers of a new profession. They will create a demand for a grade of service which can only be adequately supplied by charity training schools.[8]

It was not until 1897 that Miss Richmond, in a paper given before the Section on Organization of Charity at the National Conference, presented her proposal for a charity training school. "We owe it," she said, "to those who shall come after us that they shall be spared the groping and blundering by which we have acquired our own stock of experience." She reminded her colleagues that the charity organization societies had always stood for trained service in charity, at least in theory, and yet had done little or nothing to supply the demand they had created. "The question now is," she said, "how to get educated young men and women to make a life vocation of charity organization work." And her answer was, "We must educate them." Then she gave a "rough sketch" of a training school. The first step was to find the right man to organize it, a university-trained man who believed that a training school for charity workers—not just for charity organization workers but for all those engaged in the care of the unfortunate—is "necessary and practicable and [who] must be guaranteed time, money, and entire freedom of action, together with the hearty support of our leading charitable specialists." For the location of the school a large city would be best and it might be "that he [the headmaster] would seek connection with some institution of learning, though it should never be forgotten that the emphasis is to be put on practical work rather than on academic requirements. Vital connection, there-fore, would of necessity be made with the public and private chari-ties of the city." Only through such a school offering courses for relief workers, child-saving agents, and other charitable specialists would it be possible, she felt, for "those who are doctoring social diseases in many departments of charitable work [to find] a common ground of agreement, and be forced to recognize certain established principles as underlying all effective service." [9]

To judge by the recorded discussion at the National Conference, Miss Richmond's suggestions received a somewhat mixed reception. Frances R. Morse, a board member from Boston who was later to serve on the advisory committee of the School of Social Work in Boston, in a letter to Miss Richmond had expressed many doubts as to the desirability of a "normal school" for charity workers, although "oddly enough . . . someone here [in Boston] had just pro-posed something of a like nature." She feared that "we should get a somewhat academic and opinionated graduate" and that "young men and women who had gone through a two-years' course would feel too much that they knew all that could be learned." Others felt that what was already available in the way of college courses was enough, at least for the time being, and, while recognizing the need for a school, thought it attainable only in the remote future, after the public had been brought to "understand that a person who enters philanthropic work is entitled to consideration, to recognition as a part of the social fabric." In other words, they felt a training school was not practicable until a professional standard had been established.[10]

Miss Richmond's attitude that "we can never acquire a professional standard until we have a school" was shared by Edward T. Devine, executive of the New York Charity Organization Society, and in 1898 that society with the strong support of its board and of its president, Robert W. deForest, launched the New York School of Philanthropy (now the New York School of Social Work of Columbia University), the first in the United States.

Josephine Shaw Lowell served as a member of the school's advisory committee and until her death in 1905 gave occasional lectures. Mary Richmond was for years an active participant in the teaching program, traveling from Baltimore and later from Philadelphia until her work settled her permanently in New York. Philip W. Ayres, who had studied under Amos Warner at Johns Hopkins and had had an active training program as secretary in Cincinnati, was appointed director of the school. The part-time faculty included many of the leaders in social work from other cities as well as from New York. A number of professors from college or university departments of philosophy, sociology, and ethics were also invited to lecture from time to time.

For the first six years the school limited its program to a six-week summer course. In 1904 it inaugurated a full academic year and continued the summer session as an institute primarily for employed workers. Eventually a two-year curriculum was developed and in 1940 it became a graduate school of Columbia University, although it continued its connection with the New York society until 1950.

No other charity organization society conducted a professional school but many played an active part in getting schools started and in their development, furnishing trustees and faculty as well as supervised practice for students. The number of schools increased slowly and the acceptance of a full two-year course of graduate study came even more slowly. As a rule the schools followed the plan of "didactic instruction" in the classroom and supervised practice in agencies, usually in two different ones. The students received a much more rounded training than was possible under the apprentice system, which, however, continued for a good many years. Even today the schools, numbering more than fifty approved by the Council on Social Work Education, have far too few graduates to meet the demand for qualified workers.

Developing Social Work Literature

Whether the training was to be in schools or by the apprentice method, there was an urgent and continuing need for material that could be used in teaching. In the twenty years between the founding of the first charity organization society and the launching of the School of Philanthropy in New York City there had been some valuable additions to the literature on charity, notably *American Charities* by Amos G. Warner, published in 1894.[11] It had been quickly adopted as a textbook in agencies and colleges. Several new periodicals had been started. *Lend a Hand,* published in Boston, was concerned with the whole field of philanthropy. *Charities,* which later became *Charities and The Commons* and still later *The Survey,* was originally published by the Charity Organization Society of New York City but was not limited to New York either in its content or its circulation. A less ambitious magazine, *The Charities Record* published by the Baltimore Charity Organization Society, had a good deal of material on method as well as on subjects of general interest.

The beginnings of the settlement house movement in this country —at Hull House, established in Chicago in 1889, and at the Henry Street Settlement, established in New York in 1893—were described in such books as *Hull House Maps and Papers,*[12] and *How the Other Half Lives* by Jacob Riis,[13] and gave fresh insight into some of the problems with which the societies were struggling.

The charity organization leaders also used material from other professions—particularly education, medicine, and law—and drew on the rich sources of human experience in biography, history, novels, and poetry. Edward T. Devine said in 1899, "We make it our aim at the same time to improve our methods, to gather from all sources the results of experience, to embody them so far as practicable in definite and tangible precedents for the guidance of ourselves and others so as to build up incidentally what may be called the rudiments of a science of charity." [14]

The opening of the schools stimulated the development of agency material suitable for teaching and highlighted the need for improvement in case recording. Although the records were inadequate and continued to be so for many years, maximum use was made of them in training staff and in attempting to clarify method and to evaluate the work being done. Many of the annual reports, especially those of the larger and older societies, gave detailed case stories and explained what Amos Warner called "the countless things . . . which are necessary in wisely aiding the poor." [15] In *The Charities Record,* of Baltimore, one executive is quoted as writing to another, "We find our best teacher to be the experience of older societies. Your last report not only gives us a fund of information but is a means of education as well." In the 1899 report of the Baltimore society, its secretary, Mary Richmond, presented the results of a comprehensive study based on case records of the effects of the work of the society on family life in poor homes. "The obstacles to normal family life are briefly considered, then illustrations are given of the society's efforts to remove these obstacles, not omitting a frank statement of failures."

At the same time that she was preparing the 1899 annual report Miss Richmond was working on *Friendly Visiting Among the Poor, A Handbook for Charity Workers.* [16] The book, like the report, "treats of various aspects of the home life of the poor as affected by charity." It was a practical guide for all charity visitors—not just for those of the charity organization society—but its focus was on "the organization of the poor man's home rather than the organization of charity." An analysis of the role of each member of the family group was followed by a description of individual needs and of the roles of the visitor and the community in meeting those needs. Paid workers, as well as the volunteers to whom the book was addressed, found it valuable, but the author made quite clear her feeling that "professional visiting can never be friendly." The paid worker's job was different though not less important; the facts needed in order to know how to help a family are "best filled in by a competent trained agent rather than by the friendly visitor, whose relations with the family render searching inquiry difficult and often undesirable." *Friendly Visiting* represented the integration of principles and practices which the charity organization movement had long needed and for which Mary Richmond had an unusual gift.

The next few years saw the publication of a number of books based on the work of the charity organization societies. Among them were: *The Practice of Charity* (1901), *The Principles of Relief* (1904), *Misery and Its Causes* (1909), all by Edward T. Devine; [17] *The Good Neighbor in the Modern City* (1907) by Mary E. Richmond; [18] and *The Charity Visitor* (1918) by Amelia Sears.[19] Other fields of social work also made valuable additions to the meager literature of the profession. But for some years the only contributions to casework literature were in the form of pamphlets focused on some aspect of day-by-day practice. Social work was going through a period when measures for social reform had more appeal than had the slower methods of helping individuals, and the necessity for studying the interplay between the two processes, which charity organization had demonstrated earlier, was frequently lost sight of. The clarification and strengthening of casework skills were urgently needed.

Study of Case Records

A beginning was now made in the direction of study of case records. In 1905, a group of charity organization societies had set up a plan for the exchange of forms, publicity, and so on, to be carried on by the Field Department of the magazine, *Charities and The Commons*. A committee of the Field Department, acting on the conviction that workers could learn from seeing what societies other than their own were doing, collected case records, which were carefully disguised, from forty-five charity organization societies. These, together with sample face sheets (called "case cards") and other forms, were placed on display at the National Conference at its 1908 session at Richmond, Virginia. At the Conference, Francis H. McLean, field secretary of the Field Department, expressed more concern about the quality of the work than the manner of recording:

> Many of the cases . . . did not lack at all in thoroughness of investigation. Every possible source of information was approached, and yet one reached the end with a sense of disappointment. . . . The closely

48

typewritten pages were a rebuke to any accusation of lack of bulk. Yet what did the record lack? It lacked the breath of life! . . . A sane, clear, alert recognition . . . of what were the most significant and important things to be learned. . . . Fussing and fussing on with a case for months . . . is not *prima facie* evidence that we are actually treating it.[20]

The report also pointed out that investigation, one of the skills on which charity organization had prided itself, was not the pursuit of evidence to prove that a person was lying, not "the accumulation of corroborative details, not a collection of material as the ashman gathers ashes," but a creative search for the possibilities of people and it called for workers with "social imagination that is dynamic, not static. . . . So dignify more and more your investigations, making them more nearly vibrant with the pulse of human life, more true, more helpful, more inspiring toward the best development [of a human being]."

The case record exhibit, which became an annual affair and has continued down to the present under the national association, was an important factor in the development of casework, since it offered the opportunity for the "full and free comparison of methods," thus helping to establish and maintain comparable standards among the agencies.

An even more important undertaking was the preparation of selected case records, mimeographed or printed, for use in training students and workers. This also was sponsored by the Field Department. Under the title *The Real Story of a Real Family*, Mary Richmond gave the history of work with a widow and her four children over a nine-year period, from 1898 to 1907. A prefatory note acknowledges that the work presented is far from perfect: "In the publication of this and other actual case records neither the societies from which they come nor the Field Department offer them as model records. Rather are they offered as being suggestive, through study and criticism, in realizing that standard of thorough work in investigation and treatment which we are striving to reach. There are both weak points and debatable points in the record herewith presented." Occasional footnotes point out some of the many weaknesses or suggest questions for discussion. At the end of the record there is a definite request for criticism to be sent to the Department:

"There may be criticism of various points of this record. If so, one purpose in publishing it will have been accomplished."

The case record exhibit and the teaching records provided a means for a large number of societies to contribute to the improvement in methods which was gradually taking place. More important still, the Field Department was given a chance to examine a cross-section of what was probably the best work then being done. Taken as a whole the work was uneven in quality, varying greatly from agency to agency, and showing many weaknesses. Some of the latter doubtless were due to heavy case loads and lack of time but some, it was soon clear, were due to lack of knowledge of how to do the work, to complete ignorance of the techniques of investigation and treatment. In the Field Department *Bulletin* of January, 1909, Mr. McLean asks, "How could it be otherwise? Where are the published volumes dealing with [method]? What is our present method? We pitchfork our new workers into the field and tell them to find their own way." Fortunately, a few workers had shown a rare ability in evolving and formulating techniques and had taught them to others. It was to these that a Field Department request was directed, asking them to put the fundamentals of the method "into recorded form for the benefit alike of old and new workers. We say old workers, of whom we are one, because, while experience is a good teacher there is no surety that it will be a thorough teacher."

Plans were outlined for a series of articles on investigation, interviewing, and case recording, to be printed in the *Bulletin*, to be followed later by articles on treatment, with full recognition that no "series of articles on technique [would], in itself, make good investigators" but should provide the groundwork upon which to build. The articles were informal, most of them written by practicing caseworkers. Included in the series, which ran in nine issues of the *Bulletin*, were papers by a physician, a lawyer, a historian, and a professor of literature, each contributing to the technique of investigation from the point of view of his specialty. The outline of the project included a section on the art of case recording which was planned as "an attempt to show the way to better case writing, something better than a boggy morass. Much good work is lost in poor case writing, lost to the detriment of the families involved as well as to the communities." This section of the project as well as some of the others had not been completed when the Field Department of *Charities and The Commons* became part of the Charity Organization Department of the Russell Sage Foundation in October, 1909.

The director of the new department was Mary Richmond, who continued many of the projects of the previous Field Department. Renewed effort was made to put the fundamental techniques into recorded form. A printed monthly *Bulletin* carried articles on interviewing, case recording, and other aspects of casework. These, like most of the earlier articles in the Field Department *Bulletin,* were written by practitioners. They were to be "all first hand material hammered out of personal experience," as a part of an effort "to work out together, a plan of more effectual helpfulness for victims of misfortune. . . . No one of us can claim any large amount of knowledge as yet as to the right way in which to proceed."

Annual Training Institute

Miss Richmond's recognition of the great need of something more than printed material to supplement apprentice training and the training offered by the few schools of social work—plus her keen interest in teaching—led her to undertake a unique project which she called "short trip training." She organized and served as leader of a "Charity Organization Institute" which was held annually in New York City in the summer, from 1910 through 1922. The Institute was conducted as part of the program of the Charity Organization Department of the Russell Sage Foundation.

In the beginning the Institute was nominally under the auspices of the New York School of Philanthropy but it gave no scholastic credits and its management was in the hands of the Department. It was designed for staff members of charity organization societies in the United States and Canada. The group was limited to from twenty to twenty-five members selected each year from a much larger number of applications, with special attention to representation from both large and small cities and from various geographical regions. The sessions were conducted as seminars with committee assignments and study projects. According to a report of the 1910 Institute in the Charity Organization Department *Bulletin,* the emphasis was "upon the co-operative nature of charity organization work, upon its close interrelation with health questions, industrial questions, the conditions surrounding childlife, the drift of populations and the administration of public departments."

Miss Richmond, assisted by Francis H. McLean, directed the Institute until 1922, when she reluctantly decided she could not continue. She urged that it be taken over by the American Association for Organizing Family Social Work (as the national association of agencies was then called). This plan was put into effect in 1925 and the Institute was held annually under the Association's auspices through 1932, under the leadership first of Frank J. Bruno and later of Betsey Libbey, assisted by Mr. McLean and other members of the Association staff. Thereafter the Association sponsored regional institutes as a means of stimulation and refreshment rather than training, and was able, because of decentralization, to reach a larger number of workers than it had reached through the Institute held in New York City.

Developing a Method

The Field Department of *Charities and The Commons* (1905–1909), followed by the Charity Organization Department of the Russell Sage Foundation (1909), and later by the National Association of Societies for Organizing Charity (1911), gave the agencies a greater opportunity for joint thinking and action than had hitherto been possible. The *Bulletins,* the Institutes, and various other informal conferences provided channels of communication and at the same time stimulated self-examination, analysis, and evaluation of practice, and encouraged writing on professional subjects. Some of the results were evident in the series of case histories that appeared irregularly in the Charity Organization Department *Bulletin* from 1911 to 1915. The work recorded showed marked improvement over that in the records printed earlier and the method of presentation was more effective.

This second venture in printing records for teaching purposes was based on the "growing conviction that skill in casework can be developed in large numbers of social workers in no other way than by case record study." The records were carefully disguised and, as a further protection, their distribution was limited to agencies and teachers known to the Department. The editor asked for comments and criticisms and was especially eager to get reports of staff discussions. Not only charity organization societies but social workers from other types of agencies and members of other professions were asked to read the records and comment on them. Dr. Adolph Meyer, a psychiatrist in Johns Hopkins Hospital, after a lengthy discussion of the work described in a record, expressed his keen interest in the project and added: "The literature for the social worker's instruction does not exist today [1912]. Reviewing the cases at hand will be the best reading for them and if there is enough pressure and enough demand the proper kind of literature will shape itself. Hence my hope that you will go on reporting actual cases."

Material for the "proper kind of literature" was slowly accumulating, partly through the *Bulletins* and the Institutes, which brought together the experience of charity organization societies in different parts of the country, partly through the study of case records made during field visits to local societies by Francis H. McLean and by others. Additional contributions were coming from caseworkers in other fields of service. The idea of the sympathetic study of the individual in his social environment as a first step in helping him—for which the charity organizationists had fought—had been adopted and adapted in other types of agencies. Medical social work, child welfare, and children's courts were making important additions to the body of knowledge and method needed by all caseworkers.

Out of the thinking and practice of a large number of workers, representing different types of agencies, which Miss Richmond painstakingly gathered and compared, came *Social Diagnosis*.[21] It was published just forty years after the launching of the first charity organization society, and was hailed as "establishing the scientific basis of a new profession." The book was designed not only for the field of charity organization—or family social work, as it was beginning to be called—but "for any social work which involves differentiation." Its material was drawn from various casework agencies as well as from other professions such as law, medicine, education. It consolidated the gains that had been made in casework method and showed the relationship of current practice to the early philosophy of charity organization—a philosophy "so sound and so inspired that science came later not to correct but to fulfil it." At the same time it looked to the future and pointed the way for continuing study. Miss Richmond herself saw the book as a beginning only, to be followed as soon as possible by carefully edited "volumes of case histories" from other pens. "It may also be predicted," she wrote, "that the forms of organization now responsible for case work will change, that its scope and skill will advance far beyond the present-day practice described in this study." Miss Richmond had pointed out how greatly casework practice could be clarified and enriched by material from other professions and added another prediction: "From applied psychology . . . we are likely to receive in the future contributions which may, in many important particulars, modify the methods described in this book. . . . There are, then," she concluded, "tasks of absorbing interest awaiting the social case workers of this and the next generation."

The hoped-for volumes of case studies were not immediately forthcoming but "tasks of absorbing interest" were. In the year in which *Social Diagnosis* was published the United States was plunged into the first world war. There was an immediate call from the Red Cross for workers and for help in training them to care for the families of men in the armed forces. Miss Richmond suggested the name "Home Service" for this work and prepared a Home Service manual setting forth the principles and methods of social casework. This manual and the later preparation of case records for training purposes, along with the enlistment of family caseworkers in the Red Cross, resulted in the extension of casework service to families and communities that had never heard of "charity organization" or "casework" and brought increased understanding of the possible uses of casework service. At the same time the needs of the emotionally disturbed soldiers during and after the war gave impetus to collaborative treatment efforts by caseworkers and psychiatrists. This new development contributed greatly to the caseworker's knowledge about human behavior and motivation. By 1918, casework, which Charles S. Loch in 1896 had called a "new social ability," was on its way to realize its possibilities as an instrument of democracy, possibilities in which Octavia Hill, Josephine Shaw Lowell, and others had ardently believed.

References

1. Robert Treat Paine, *Proceedings of the National Conference of Charities and Correction: 1881,* p. 119.
2. Oscar C. McCulloch, "Associated Charities": Report of Committee on Charitable Organization in Cities, *Proceedings, NCCC: 1880,* p. 133.
3. Zilpha D. Smith, chairman, "Organization of Charities": Report of the Committee on the Organization of Charity, *Proceedings, NCCC: 1888,* p. 127.
4. Charles D. Kellogg, "Charity Organization as an Educating Force," p. 450, and "Co-operation in the Work of Charity: Internal Co-operation," p. 429, *Proceedings, NCCC: 1892.*
5. Mary E. Richmond, *The Long View,* eds. Joanna C. Colcord and Ruth Z. S. Mann, Russell Sage Foundation, New York, 1930, p. 561.
6. Albert O. Wright, "The New Philanthropy," *Proceedings, NCCC: 1896,* p. 5.
7. Amos G. Warner, *American Charities,* Thomas Y. Crowell & Co., New York, 1894, pp. 403–404.
8. Mary E. Richmond, "The Art of Asking Questions," *Baltimore Charities Record,* Vol. II, No. 5 (1896), p. 52; also *The Long View,* p. 107.
9. Mary E. Richmond, "The Need of a Training School in Applied Philanthropy," *Proceedings, NCCC: 1897,* pp. 65–79 of special volume for Section on Organization of Charities; also *The Long View,* p. 99.
10. *Ibid., Proceedings, NCCC: 1897 (supra).*
11. Warner, *op. cit.*
12. *Hull House Maps and Papers,* Thomas Y. Crowell & Co., New York, 1895.
13. Jacob Riis, *How the Other Half Lives,* Scribner, New York, 1890.
14. Edward T. Devine, "Organization of Charity," *Proceedings, NCCC: 1899,* p. 282.
15. Warner, *op. cit.,* p. 392.
16. Mary E. Richmond, *Friendly Visiting Among the Poor, A Handbook for Charity Workers,* Macmillan Co., New York, 1899.
17. Edward T. Devine: *The Practice of Charity,* Lentilhon & Co., New York, 1901; *The Principles of Relief,* Macmillan Co., New York, 1904; *Misery and Its Causes,* Macmillan Co., New York, 1909.
18. Mary E. Richmond, *The Good Neighbor in the Modern City,* J. B. Lippincott Co., Philadelphia, 1907.
19. Amelia Sears, *The Charity Visitor; A Handbook for Beginners,* School of Civics and Philanthropy, Chicago, 1918.
20. Francis H. McLean, "How May We Increase Our Standards of Efficiency in Dealing with Needy Families?," *Proceedings, NCCC: 1908,* pp. 99–110.
21. Mary E. Richmond, *Social Diagnosis,* Russell Sage Foundation, New York, 1917.

IV. Public or Private Relief

IN HIS PLANNING for the society in Buffalo, the Rev. S. Humphreys Gurteen had adopted the point of view of the London society that a charity organization society differs essentially from a relief society. Concerning the former he said, "Being primarily a medium of intercommunication between Charitable Societies, it gives no material relief except as grants or loans, and this only when such temporary assistance will ensure a permanent result." He went on to say, "There must be no relief given by the Organization itself, except in very urgent cases." [1]

Not Relief Societies

Many of the early societies felt that even such limited distribution of alms as Gurteen suggested would be a drawback to their work, tend to obscure its real character, and hinder its progress. This had happened to the associations established in the 1840's which had started out to "raise the needy above the need of relief" but, because they also gave relief when necessary, the relief function gradually submerged all others. The only way to avoid a similar fate seemed to be for the new societies to adopt constitutional provisions prohibiting the distribution of any relief from their own funds. The Boston Associated Charities had at first had a clause permitting the giving of relief if it could not be procured from any other source but the largest local relief agency

56

opposed this proviso and the line was, as Robert Treat Paine of the Associated Charities expressed it, "stricken out by the hand of God." He considered this action fortunate because it left the society free to give its attention to problems of the permanent welfare of families. The constitution of the New York Charity Organization Society also prohibited relief from its own funds and the model constitutions advocated by Josephine Shaw Lowell and later by Edward T. Devine stipulated, "This society shall not give relief from its own funds."

In 1887 Charles D. Kellogg, executive of the New York Charity Organization Society, reporting to the National Conference of Charities and Correction, found that "in some localities material relief from funds at its [the Charity Organization Society's] disposal has been a deplored necessity, which must be reduced to a secondary incident of the work, or, better still, entirely abolished." [2]

In 1893, answers to questionnaires sent to societies indicated that more than 50 per cent of those that reported did not give relief from their own funds, although it must be borne in mind that not all existing societies answered. It was generally accepted, at least in theory, that, as Oscar C. McCulloch of Indianapolis told the National Conference in 1889, "the more a society depends upon physical relief, and the more of a fund it has to dispense, the less will it resort to its great fundamental principle of helping a man to help himself." [3] Amos G. Warner of Baltimore, who had been executive of a charity organization society and a teacher of sociology, supported the "no relief" point of view: "Experience seems to have shown that this abstention from relief-giving has been the very best thing to allay the jealousy of older societies; and not only this, but that it has been the salvation of charity organization societies, preserving them for the higher purposes which they had in view." [4]

At the same time the question of whether a charity organization society should give relief was not to be confused with the question of whether relief should be given. It was the plan of these societies that they would organize relief or co-ordinate the relief giving of other agencies or raise money to use as needed on a case-by-case basis. They would demonstrate the way to give relief so that it would fit the individual situation and stimulate the recipient to

57

self-help or, best of all, they would provide help that would remedy the difficulty without resorting to material aid. Seth Low, of the newly organized Brooklyn Bureau of Charities, explained that, when economic help outside an institution—usually referred to as "outdoor relief"—was unavoidable, "Private benevolence seems preferable to public relief, because it is almost always inspired by a higher motive, and therefore more apt to consider the good of the receiver, because it contains within itself the limits to which it can be carried and because such relief is less readily sought after by the recipients." [5]

Status of Public Relief

Many of the criticisms of public outdoor relief in the 1870's and 1880's were apparently justified. In the opinion of the National Conference Committee on the Prevention of Pauperism, 1885, "The admixture of politics with public charity is the great evil of our American system, and is more dangerous here, from the form of our national institutions, than in most other countries." [6] Officials in charge of "poor relief" were usually elected for short terms, paid sometimes on the basis of the number of people aided, sometimes a purely nominal salary. They did not have to have any special qualifications either of education or experience. To quote Seth Low again: "In some States, or sections of States, the office of Overseer of the Poor is at the bottom of the political ladder. The Overseers are . . . expected to serve party or personal ends." [7] The relief given was inadequate in amount, was granted without inquiry as to real need, and was unaccompanied by any effort to discover and change the conditions that had caused the need.

Other reasons advanced against public outdoor relief included the belief, stated by Charles D. Kellogg, that the "mere existence of an appropriation from the public treasury was demoralizing to the poor, who thought they had a right to share in it"; [8] that such a fund dried up the sources of private beneficence and, as stated by Frederic Almy, general secretary of the Buffalo society, checked "the growth of the more sympathetic, more personal and helpful work of private charity." [9] Another argument sometimes advanced was that appropriations for public outdoor relief would mean less money for public institutions, which were a legitimate responsibility of the municipality. Most, if not all, of the early charity organization societies were agreed that the existing system was expensive from a monetary point of view, and harmful to those for whose help it was intended. There was, however, a wide difference of opinion as to what should be done to improve the situation.

In a report to the National Conference in 1881, Dr. Charles E. Cadwalader, board member of the Philadelphia society, said: "It is claimed by some good authorities that it would be better for these appropriations [for public outdoor relief], as they are now administered, to cease altogether; that private charity is equal to all just demands, and that what municipalities donate annually is likely to have a pauperizing instead of a beneficial effect. On the other hand it is argued that to unite with the city authorities is the best way of securing the co-operation of the authorities. . . . There is, after all, nothing so trustworthy as experience, and the varied experiments now being tried in the different cities ought eventually to furnish a satisfactory settlement of this question." [10]

The idea of doing away with the system found strong advocates, particularly in the cities where public outdoor relief was no longer in use. It was abolished in Brooklyn in 1878 because it had been found to have no support in law, although its wasteful and corrupt administration were also strong arguments against it. The Brooklyn Bureau of Charities was organized later in that same year. Philadelphia had discontinued appropriations for outdoor relief in 1879, some said as a retaliation against the criticisms implied in the establishment of the Society for Organizing Charity the previous year. In neither city had the discontinuance resulted in the anticipated increase in applications to institutions or to private charity. Beginning in 1876, public outdoor relief in New York City was limited to annual allowances to the blind, distribution of coal in winter, and medical relief. Neither Baltimore nor Washington, D. C., gave any public outdoor relief. Some charity organizationists argued that, if these large cities could manage without provision for economic help from public funds outside of institutions, it seeemed desirable to work toward the same objective in all cities.

There were some, however, who questioned such drastic measures. The Rev. H. C. Duganne of the Lowell (Massachusetts) Associated

59

Charities wondered whether the state or municipality had the right to shirk responsibility for the care of its poor and throw the burden upon benevolence. He pointed out that the state tax was borne by all while voluntary agencies were supported by a few. He deplored the fact that municipal relief had exaggerated the evils it had sought to correct. He believed it should not be abolished but should be restricted both as to amounts and to periods of continuance:

> I think it is not the thing that needs to be abolished, but the methods. There seems to be no good reason why these should not be so modified and changed as to make municipal relief, when administered to the same class, as efficient and beneficial as that given by many, and perhaps most, of our voluntary agencies. . . . Voluntary agencies have been unwisely administered and have also done mischief in the way of pauper making. It matters little from what source the relief comes, if it comes too freely and is continued too long.[11]

Relationships with Public Relief Departments

Relations of some sort between charity organization societies and public outdoor relief departments, where such existed, were of course inevitable. Efforts to abolish the outdoor relief system were few and did not meet with success, although in some cities the total expenditures for public relief were gradually reduced. Acceptance of the status quo and exchange of information, usually on the initiative of the private agency, were fairly common. In some instances the charity organization method of investigation was thought to have been a good influence on the administration of public relief, even when the society had not undertaken an aggressive reform program. Public relief officials were invited to membership on district or case committees and charity organization board members served on the committees of the municipal charities.

The Indianapolis society first hoped to abolish public outdoor relief but later devoted its efforts to securing immediate and more adequate relief for those eligible. Oscar McCulloch reported to the National Conference in 1880 that the Council or Executive Committee of the Indianapolis Charity Organization Society "watches the public administration of relief; conducts its independent system of investigation and recommends or criticizes the official action of the Overseers of the Poor." [12]

The Boston society appointed a board Committee on Municipal

Charities and Correction to make suggestions for improvement, and in 1883 Erving Winslow reported that the committee had "invoked the aid of the voluntary labors of private individuals in all the official agencies of relief." [13]   Frances R. Morse, another board member from Boston, felt that the "charity organization habit of mind should help us to keep on the look out for all wise means of social improvement . . . to try wherever we can to help forward the admirable and often unobserved work of . . . the subordinate officers of Overseers of the Poor." [14]

A few family agencies undertook to improve matters by investigating all applicants for public relief. The Buffalo society continued this practice for more than forty years. In most cities supplementation of the always inadequate public relief was fairly common practice and in these situations the charity organization society tried to meet other needs as well as to give economic aid. Another type of "co-operation" was for the voluntary agency to investigate and make recommendations to the poor-relief official, who then issued an order or a check. From this dubious arrangement it was but a step to the even worse practice of allowing the charity organization society to take full charge of the disbursing of public relief funds. This lump-sum subsidy plan was considered dangerous by most of the leaders in charity organization.

Amos G. Warner, who was Commissioner of Public Charities of the District of Columbia, told the National Conference in 1892, "No private association for organizing charity should receive any subsidy from the public funds of the city, county, or State." [15]   The plan was practiced intermittently, however, in a number of communities over a period of years, usually to the disadvantage of both the governmental and the voluntary agency. The relief load as a rule was too heavy for the understaffed private agency to handle adequately and the demonstrations, by which the agencies had hoped to educate the community to the value of skill in the administration of relief, failed to materialize.

The London Charity Organisation Society had seen the fallacy of any joint arrangement. Charles S. Loch had said: "To utilize and improve [poor relief] according to the lines of its development, is a first duty with those who would organize charity. . . . It follows that charity organization will promote co-operation between the administration of public relief and the administration of charitable funds so that each body, by a division of labor, may fulfill its own function." [16] Gurteen also had advocated this principle and Seth Low, who was strongly in favor of doing away with public outdoor relief altogether, still felt that "one of the first things organization in charity seeks to accomplish is to harmonize these public and private efforts at outdoor relief." [17]

Attempts at harmonizing the public and private efforts resulted in a number of different plans for division of labor. From the Boston publication, *Lend a Hand,* it is learned that as early as 1885 the Boston Associated Charities asked the Overseers of the Poor to send the private agency all the persons who were asking for help for the first time, partly to keep them from the disgrace of being on the "poor books," partly to see whether some help other than relief along with personal service might meet their needs. This plan of having private charity take the first applications was favored by many of the agencies. Alexander Johnson, secretary of the State Board of Charities in Indianapolis, commented on it at the International Congress of Charities, Correction, and Philanthropy, at Chicago in 1893:

> The charity organization society is . . . able to propose plans of co-operation to the overseer of the poor which he can accept with confidence. . . . Mutual delimitation of work is one of the most practical and useful [plans]. . . . For instance, a charity organization society says to the overseer of the poor, "We will take the responsibility for all new cases, send them to us without investigation, you may still help those on the poor books; let us keep the new cases off them, for once on it is hard to get them off again." A more usual form [of co-operation] is when the charity organization society takes all the cases which only a strained construction of the law allows the overseer to help, and yet whose necessity seems so great that he feels they need and must have aid. It [co-operation] means more than an agreement to do certain work or leave it undone. It means hearty, cordial sympathy, wise help and true encouragement. [18]

Other leaders urged flexible rather than routine arrangements and an understanding of the problems common to both types of agency. At the International Congress in Chicago Mary Richmond said:

> The question of the demarcation of private and public charity is, after all, a question of expediency, and I cannot formulate any one great moral principle that is involved in the division of work. If it is simply

62

a question of expediency do not let us get into the habit of feeling that private and public charities are in any sense opposed to each other. I think that is a possible tendency and a very fatal one. It has occurred to me that one function of a charity organization society may well be to create an intelligent public interest in public charities. No public charity can be a success without that. Public officials are just like other people. Unless they have someone interested in what they are doing, their interest flags. . . . A charity organization society is only doing the right thing when it puts its members into right relations with every other charity in the community, public and private.[19]

A few societies were making progress in bringing to bear upon the public charities "the best intelligence and conscience of the community" and were slowly developing good relations between agencies. At the National Conference in 1890 the Portland, Maine, Associated Charities reported a decided improvement in the administration of official relief, and the society in Fall River, Massachusetts, stated its expectation of obtaining an appointive board of Overseers of the Poor. At the National Conference in 1897, James R. Wylie reported that in 1895 the charity organization society of Grand Rapids, Michigan, had initiated legislative action for "an amendment of our charter . . . providing for the appointment by the Mayor . . . of a non-political board of poor commissioners, who would serve without compensation and have exclusive charge of all matters pertaining to the care of the city poor. This law went into effect and commissioners appointed under it took charge of the department May 1, 1896." [20]

During this same period other charity organization societies continued to resist the idea of public outdoor relief, especially in those cities where the system had been abolished or limited. A bill to provide support for widows with children in New York City was introduced in the state legislature in 1897 but failed to pass because of the strong opposition of the New York Charity Organization Society and the State Charities Aid Association. Under this bill "any child in an institution might be returned to its parents by the New York Society for the Prevention of Cruelty to Children. The city controller thereafter was to pay to the parents through the SPCC the same amount of money that the institution had been receiving." [21] The social agencies that opposed the bill recognized the soundness of the principle that children should not be separated from their parents for economic reasons only. They also accepted the fact that aid to widows and children was not "evil," as were some other types of relief, but they still felt that these families should be kept off the poor books lest the children grow up as paupers. The main objections to the bill, however, were not against public outdoor relief in general, but were based on two main points: first, that the bill was illegal since, under the New York City Charter, adopted in 1897, outdoor relief from city funds was limited to pensions to the blind; second, that it was unsound to place the management of public funds in the hands of a private agency. In addition the Charity Organization Society contended that private resources were adequate to meet existing needs.

Efforts to Improve Public Relief

In 1900, Frederic Almy of Buffalo, who had been among the most uncompromising opponents of public outdoor relief, came forward with what was, for him, a new point of view: "Private charity can be just as vicious and pauperizing, just as wasteful, just as corrupt and profligate, as public charity. If public almsgiving with no investigation or with no intelligence is bad, why not reform it instead of doing away with it? To acquiesce supinely in a debauching city government, and to attempt to organize a private agency to do the city's work is a surrender of manhood. . . . If well-administered city relief is best, reform your civil service and make such relief your goal." [22] At the same meeting, George S. Wilson, general secretary of the Washington, D. C. society, although still convinced that even the best public outdoor relief was less desirable than private, recognized that "if the charity organization societies cannot bring about the abolition of [public] outdoor relief in the immediate future, there still rests upon them the responsibility of using their efforts to bring about the best possible administration of the system." [23]

Along with these more liberal attitudes toward public outdoor relief, charity organization societies were beginning to free themselves from an almost superstitious fear of relief giving. Not all of the societies gave relief from their own funds but Frederic Almy could report in 1904 that "the reaction of private charity against largess, or alms, was for a time excessive. . . . Charity organization societies have begun to realize this, and they are steadily placing more emphasis upon the value of relief and less upon its dangers." [24] They were also considering what they meant by adequate relief, which they had supported as a principle but which had been difficult to apply in practice. In Buffalo, for example, it was not until 1908 that plans for realistic budgeting of relief were finally developed.

From time to time there were definite suggestions as to ways in which the weaknesses in the administration of public relief so often complained of could be corrected. It was proposed that public departments as well as charity organization societies use voluntary workers for personal service to relief recipients but it was noted that these departments must have community support if they were to achieve higher standards. Jeffrey R. Brackett spoke to the National Conference of 1903 on this subject:

> Let us at least ask for full information of the best work being done with families and individuals by public officials. . . . The best way to get good work done . . . is to plead for a high standard and ask for results. . . . If all that is expected of men is to administer doles, will not most of them rest satisfied with giving doles; and how will you then get the best men to be officials, men who will do away with doles? Such information will help us to learn what processes will most tend to the doing away of the public aid that harms, to the spending of more time and thought by public officials on needed institutional care, and to the development of personal service, of the highest form of charity for needy families.[25]

In 1904 Professor C. R. Henderson wrote optimistically of progress in harmonizing public and private outdoor relief: "Gradually it has been made evident that public and private charity are not rivals but parts of one system, and that they complement each other, both being necessary. Hence there are everywhere efforts to define the appropriate fields of public and private agencies and to promote a good understanding and effective co-operation between them." He suggested that public outdoor relief should be responsible for cases where careful control of personal conduct was necessary and that private charity should care for those where free activity was desirable.[26]

It is indicative of the persistence of widely differing points of view that, in a book published in the same year as Dr. Henderson's,

Edward T. Devine, general secretary of the New York Charity Organization Society, marshaled a formidable and, it seemed to him, conclusive array of arguments against public outdoor relief. He stated that "private philanthropy is a safer, more stable, and more generous source of supply than taxation," and, further, that the state should provide institutional care as needed and would leave to "private individuals and voluntary associations all material assistance required in the homes of the poor. . . . Private charity has naturally, or certainly may have, more elasticity, more freedom from arbitrary restrictions, and a higher standard of trained professional service." [27]

The general trend, however, was toward co-operation with public departments rather than their abolition. There had always been some who felt, as did F. H. Wines, of the Illinois State Board of Public Charities, that "the abolition of all public outdoor relief is in itself as crude a remedy for the administration of this form of relief as was the burning of the bamboo huts of the Chinese . . . in order to roast the suckling pigs." [28] The persons who had advocated abolition of outdoor relief were discovering that their efforts had not met with success. In Brooklyn and New York City the public relief system was abolished before the societies in those cities were organized and in Philadelphia the influence of the Society for Organizing Charity had been indirect. In some cities the efforts to reduce expenditures for public outdoor relief and to bring about improvement in administration had brought appreciable results, but little factual information was available about the status of public relief the country over.

In 1907 an effort to interest some of the charity organization societies in gathering material on this subject was made by Mary Richmond in a letter to members of the Exchange Branch, operated by the Field Department of *Charities and The Commons*:

> A new line of work has been suggested to our department on which I should like the advice of the co-operating societies. Many of these societies are in cities where there is no public outdoor relief, but public outdoor relief is after all the rule and not the exception in the country at large. Some of us have felt for a long time that an impartial investigation of public outdoor relief methods planned to cover several states in different parts of the country and with different social conditions might be made a useful basis for many needed reforms in the next

ten years. If data enough could be furnished to convince the Carnegie Institution or the Sage Foundation of the value of such an investigation it might be possible to persuade one or the other to finance the plan. What co-operation could your society give in furnishing such preliminary data, looking at the matter not from the point of view of your own particular city but of the whole state? Are you in favor of the Field Department's undertaking the agitation for such an investigation, or does it seem to you quite outside our province? The question at issue, of course, is not whether public relief is good or bad in itself but to secure, if possible, an impartial investigation of its present administration.

There is no evidence that this proposal was ever carried out but the interest of the Field Department in the relations between charity organization societies and public departments led to the gathering of material from local societies and its circulation through the Field Department *Bulletins*. One such statement from Mary L. Birtwell, general secretary of the Associated Charities in Cambridge, Massachusetts, in 1908, described a working arrangement that was probably fairly common where co-operative relationships had been developed: "The most earnest advocates of public outdoor relief do not deny the advantages of private over public for widows with children. . . . We encourage the ambition of the family for higher standards by taking them off the pauper list." However, the report concluded, when the need was more than the private agency could meet, responsibility was left with the Overseer of the Poor, and the Associated Charities sent a friendly visitor to give sympathetic advice and encouragement to the mother and children.

Programs for Widows' Pensions

This preference for private charity rather than public relief for widows with dependent children was strongly endorsed by the White House Conference on Dependent Children held in 1919, which did much to stimulate interest in adequate care for children and in the conservation of the home as "the highest and finest product of civilization." The leaders of the movements already under way for widows' or mothers' pensions (so-called) gained support and inspiration from the Conference but they were convinced that the pensions should come from public, not private, funds. The first state-wide law providing "Funds to Parents" was enacted in Illinois in 1911; by 1913 the total number of states with such provisions had mounted to seventeen. The bills were generally passed without consultation with social workers, public or private. Massachusetts was the first state to preface mothers' pension legislation with a study of existing conditions and in that state social workers did participate in drafting the bill that was finally passed.

For the most part, charity organization leaders were opposed, not to the idea of support for mothers and children, but to the kinds of provisions that were being advocated. They argued that the term "pension" was a euphemism for what was really a form of outdoor relief. Some felt that the task could not be done well under public administration and that, as in all public outdoor relief, the receipt of such payments would be degrading to the recipients. At the same time, many of the societies agreed that private relief resources were woefully inadequate. Frederic Almy of Buffalo, although opposed to public pensions, dissented, at least in part, from those opposed to all public relief programs. At the National Conference in 1912 he said:

> Times change . . . and I am not willing to believe that in this day public outdoor relief cannot be successful. It weighs with me that the equally delicate work of child placing is successfully done by public charity though the arguments against it would be similar. Over and over private charity has blazed the way for what became public safely after standards had been developed and established. . . . The curse of the old name of city outdoor relief is something and the new and better associations will make it easier to keep up the new and better standards.[29]

Others felt that providing widows' pensions was a partial remedy for conditions that could only be met by social insurance. Max Senior, director of United Jewish Charities in Chicago, spoke at the same meeting:

> Don't let us be satisfied with what is partial. . . . Let us nail our colors to the mast and insist on what we have been asking for these many years, the full program: insurance against industrial accident, insurance against sickness, insurance against old age, insurance against invalidity, and compulsory insurance against all these in every state of the Union.[30]

Once the laws were in effect, however, charity organization and other social workers undertook to help rather than hinder the programs, although what they could do depended on the local situation. In Chicago, Judge Merritt W. Pinckney of the Juvenile Court,

68

who was in charge of administering the Funds to Parents Act in Cook County, called together an advisory committee representing twenty of the prominent private agencies to help interpret problems to the community and to provide a case committee. In another Illinois county the judge invited representatives of the Associated Charities, visiting nurses, and another agency to serve as advisers. In some states, legislation provided for appointive committees and the use of volunteers, thus demonstrating that—as had been suggested earlier—there was no reason why public officials should not utilize methods that had proven helpful in the relief of distress by private agencies.

In Pennsylvania the law provided that the administration of the fund in each county should be in the hands of from five to seven women trustees appointed annually by the governor, with power to employ paid staff. Within the first year of operation the Allegheny County Board had employed a worker trained in the local Associated Charities. In time a number of workers with charity organization training recognized the challenge of the new provisions and accepted employment in the administration of the programs, introducing charity organization principles and methods and, at the same time, enriching their own skills. One successful administrator in a mothers' aid program, who had had long experience in family social work, wrote of her experience:

> Determining legal eligibility as a right for clients was, of course, a new approach. Separating the actual giving of relief from service was also a new approach. No case worker ever handled the financial assistance to clients in mothers' aid [in this particular program.] Once eligibility was established, the checks were mailed direct to the clients by the state and county treasurers. While eligibility was a legal matter, the case work approach learned from family case work was used. Following the establishment of eligibility the treatment was on a case work basis. There was a recognition on the part of the case workers that many clients, once their financial needs were met, were able to function quite adequately with little supervision, while others presented serious problems in various areas. [From a personal letter.]

Not all the mothers' aid programs employed caseworkers and often the co-operative relationships with charity organization and other private agencies were not desired or achieved. The actual administration of the provisions was beset with problems both for the public officials and for private agencies, as well as for the

69

mothers with dependent children and for the community as a whole. The appropriations for the programs were insufficient to care for all those who were eligible; hence there were waiting lists. The grants, limited by law, were usually meager and insufficient to provide for basic needs. Should the private family society take care of those on the waiting list? Should it supplement the grants and, if so, on what basis should it select those it would help? Should it withhold relief from those on the waiting list, refuse to supplement it and thus try to force the state to carry the responsibility it had assumed in theory though not in fact? There were advocates of each of these procedures and some efforts to get increased appropriations, but for the most part attempts to improve matters were isolated and not too successful.

Renewed Interest in Improving Public Relief

The suggestion made by Miss Richmond in 1907 that charity organization societies should acquaint themselves with the conditions and functions of public outdoor relief had brought little response. Six years later, in an article in *The Survey,* she made an even more urgent plea for the private societies to gather and interpret information about the whole public welfare program, including mothers' aid legislation and administration:

> Have we not, for the most part, turned our backs upon the administrators of public outdoor relief . . . and busied ourselves about everything under the sun rather than about their work? The danger of new and conflicting public relief authorities is obvious enough. . . . But what do . . . we . . . know about the old machinery? . . . Content with a general suspicion that the work was not being done very well, we have not thought its processes worthy of study, and now a new public outdoor relief is impending . . . but for neither the new nor the old have we any basis of fact—statistical or otherwise—to show the extent of the needs that it aims to meet, the probable cost . . . the fundamental conditions of success, the qualifications necessary in those who are to bring this success about, or the relation of the whole process to the other functions of government. . . . Should we not bestir ourselves, community by community, to discover what is happening to this fundamental work for families? [And] strive to create in each community something more than a perfunctory interest in the task of the outdoor relief official? [31]

Opportunities for gathering material about local conditions, for evaluation and exchange of experience, were considerably increased by the establishment of a national association of charity organization societies in 1911. (See Chapter V.) Francis H. McLean, the executive of the new organization, had a wide acquaintance with both private and public welfare. In his previous experience as executive of the Charity Organization Society of Montreal, a city that had neither indoor nor outdoor public relief, he had discovered that many of the traditional arguments for building up private agencies and discontinuing public welfare were not borne out in practice. He found that:

> Absence from the tax rates of compulsory benevolence has not in any way increased the generosity of the community at large with reference to charities organized into societies or institutions. . . . The simple absence of governmental responsibility works toward an unjust squandering of private charitable resources. . . . Private charity finds its interests unwholesomely centered around elemental material problems of bread and fuel. . . . Private charity has failed to perform its superadded duties satisfactorily, and its efforts have only deteriorated the character of the work which it does do. . . . Private outdoor charity . . . has possessed itself of some of the worst features of public outdoor relief as administered elsewhere; namely, stereotyped amounts of relief, that is, doles, officialism, and methods of work which mean degradation and humiliation to applicants.[32]

Mr. McLean had also worked in the Chicago United Charities, which had strongly supported a public program. His study of "The Charities of Pittsburgh" appeared in *Charities and The Commons* in 1909. It was part of the famous Pittsburgh Survey and included the public as well as the private charities. He had served as Field Director of the Field Department under *Charities and The Commons* and later under the Charity Organization Department of the Russell Sage Foundation, and in his visits to communities throughout the country he had become acquainted with the public as well as with the private agencies. In city after city he stressed the need in public departments for qualified personnel not subjected to political pressures, for the use of citizens' committees, for the keeping of records, for planned instead of planless relief, and for co-operative relations with other community agencies. Mr. McLean's recommendations and his emphasis on the responsibility of private family agencies to give support to public welfare were an outstanding contribution to what Gertrude Vaile has called the struggle "to turn repressive, old-fashioned 'poor relief' into 'family work under public auspices.' " [33]

In 1912 Gertrude Vaile, who, after her graduation from the Chicago School of Civics and Philanthropy, had worked in the Chicago United Charities, returned to her home in Denver and almost immediately was asked to serve as a member of the City Board of Charity and Correction. The next year she was appointed supervisor of relief and later executive of the Denver Department of Charities where she proceeded to put into operation the family social work methods she had learned in Chicago. Miss Vaile's first step was to suggest to her board that they call in Mr. McLean to advise about the work of the department. "At that time," Miss Vaile wrote later, "no public departments were members of the American Association of Societies for Organizing Charity and they had no claim upon the field work services of the Association. But I knew [from work in Chicago] how helpful Mr. McLean could be and he responded to my earnest request and the board's invitation to visit us." [34]

After the field visit Miss Vaile and Mr. McLean conferred by letter as long as she continued head of the department. In a letter to Miss Vaile dated October 10, 1913, Mr. McLean expressed his basic philosophy on the relations between public and private agencies:

> You see that I am reverting to the idea of a balanced system, private organization and public agency each supplementing and correcting the other, its—the private agency's—functions varying from year to year and from one public administration to another.

Miss Vaile was able to demonstrate, as others were demonstrating in mothers' aid administration, that citizens' committees, individualization of applicants, and use of volunteers were as important and as useful in the administration of public as of private relief. She felt that the public agency needed to be built on "the solid rock of intimate understanding and sympathetic backing on the part of responsible people of the general community. Friendly visitors, volunteer committees, case conferences, parlor meetings, newspaper items, co-operation with other agencies that shall be so hearty and effective that they simply can't get along without us, so that all the social work in town would just have to rise up if anything happened to us—in these things lies our only hope of stability in public outdoor relief administration." (Quoted from a personal letter from Gertrude Vaile, May, 1917.)

The work in Denver strengthened the convictions of those who already believed in the possibilities of public outdoor relief and converted many of the doubters. Frederic Almy could state in 1916: "I used to be conspicuous as an opponent of public outdoor relief, but the Denver work and other things are making me a convert to public outdoor relief where it can be made efficient. It is often well to use your energy and hard work in making public relief efficient, rather than in substituting private relief." [35] In a number of communities there were fresh efforts to give intelligent support to public welfare programs. In a few instances local committees with representatives from both public and private family agencies studied the over-all program for the care of families and made tentative recommendations for division of work.

In studies by Mr. McLean of the public departments in Rochester, New York, in 1917, and in Newark, New Jersey, and Buffalo, New York, in 1919, he recommended unpaid advisory committees, case decision committees, and qualified staff. In his Rochester report he said, "The time is passing when public social welfare departments will be satisfied with merely honest and industrious case workers; they are demanding workers with the degree of trained ability as are the private agencies." He recommended the keeping of case records, the use of the social service exchange, and agreement on a division of cases with the private family society which should be reviewed and revised from time to time. The Rochester report observed also that "in case work we cannot lay down arbitrary lines of division which will work automatically. Furthermore, it is expected that there will be give and take, and that in a very considerable number of cases public and private will be working at the same time or will work separately at different periods of treatment. Any such division as this merely indicates who should assume primary responsibility, who should assume leadership."

Mr. McLean's studies, which had been widely acclaimed, and experiences such as that in Denver, emphasized the interdependence of public and private programs and clarified the basic principles essential to sound working relationships between the two. These principles were set forth in a resolution adopted by the American

Association for Organizing Charity at the Annual Meeting of the membership at Kansas City, Missouri, in 1918:

> *Resolved,* That this Association urges its member societies to help, as opportunity offers, in the socialization of both staff and methods of work of departments of charities or other public family social work agencies; *Resolved,* That this Association believes that the division of work between public and private family work agencies, wherever the former have become socialized, cannot be defined in such terms as to be uniformly or generally applicable, but that each situation requires special study and special differentiation. However, it believes that no permanent arrangement should be on any other basis than division of cases rather than different functioning of work.

The adoption of the resolution put the charity organization societies on record as favoring more than a perfunctory interest in public welfare programs. Even though many of the societies took little or no action, the recognition of responsibility laid a foundation for later action by the Association.

References

1. S. Humphreys Gurteen, *A Handbook of Charity Organization,* published by the author, Buffalo, 1882, pp. 245, 122.
2. Charles D. Kellogg, chairman, "Organization of Charities": Report of the Committee on the Organization of Charities, *Proceedings of the National Conference of Charities and Correction: 1887,* p. 123.
3. Oscar C. McCulloch, chairman, "The Organization of Charities": Report of the Standing Committee, *Proceedings, NCCC: 1889,* p. 13.
4. Amos G. Warner, *American Charities,* Thomas Y. Crowell & Co., New York, 1894, p. 385.
5. Seth Low, "Outdoor Relief in the United States," *Proceedings, NCCC: 1881,* p. 150.
6. F. B. Sanborn, O. H. Young, R. Brinkerhoff, "The Prevention of Pauperism": Report of the Standing Committee, *Proceedings, NCCC: 1885,* p. 405.
7. Low, *op. cit.,* p. 154.
8. Charles D. Kellogg, "Charity Organization in the United States": Report of the Committee on History of Charity Organization, *Proceedings, NCCC: 1893,* p. 69.
9. Frederic Almy, "Public or Private Outdoor Relief," *Proceedings, NCCC: 1900,* p. 139.
10. Dr. Charles E. Cadwalader, chairman, "Organization of Charities in Cities": Report of the Standing Committee (based on returns from 17 of the then existing societies), *Proceedings, NCCC: 1881,* p. 107.
11. H. C. Duganne, debate on outdoor relief, *Proceedings, NCCC: 1881,* p. 155.
12. Oscar C. McCulloch, "Associated Charities": Report of Committee on Charitable Organization in Cities, *Proceedings, NCCC: 1880,* p. 129.

13. Erving Winslow, chairman, Report of Committee of Directors of Associated Charities, *Proceedings, NCCC: 1883*, pp. 94–99.

14. Frances R. Morse, "How Can We Further the Organization of Charities?," *Proceedings, NCCC: 1897*, p. 178.

15. Amos G. Warner, "Co-operation with Public Authorities," *Proceedings, NCCC: 1892*, p. 430.

16. Charles S. Loch, *Charity Organisation*, Swan Sonnenschein & Co., London, 1890, p. 18.

17. Low, *op. cit.*, p. 144.

18. Alexander Johnson, "The Co-operation of Public with Private Charitable Agencies," *Proceedings of International Congress of Charities, Correction, and Philanthropy: 1893* (Section on Charity Organization), Johns Hopkins Press, Baltimore, 1894, pp. 118–119.

19. Mary E. Richmond, *Proceedings of International Congress of Charities, Correction, and Philanthropy: 1893* (Section on Charity Organization), Johns Hopkins Press, Baltimore, 1894, p. 13.

20. James R. Wylie, "Organization of City and County Public Charities," *Proceedings, NCCC: 1897* (special volume, Section on Organization of Charities), p. 43.

21. David M. Schneider and Albert Deutsch, *The History of Public Welfare in New York State* (Vol. II), University of Chicago Press, Chicago, 1941, p. 182.

22. Frederic Almy, "Public or Private Outdoor Relief," *Proceedings, NCCC: 1900*, p. 135.

23. George S. Wilson, "Outdoor Relief in Relation to Charity Organization," *Proceedings, NCCC: 1900*, p. 261.

24. Frederic Almy, "The Use of Volunteers by Public Aid Officials," *Proceedings, NCCC: 1904*, p. 113.

25. Jeffrey R. Brackett, "The Treatment of Needy Families in Their Homes," *Proceedings, NCCC: 1903*, pp. 302–303.

26. Charles Richmond Henderson and others, *Modern Methods of Charity*, Macmillan Co., New York, 1904, p. 404.

27. Edward T. Devine, *The Principles of Relief*, Macmillan Co., New York, 1904, pp. 310–313.

28. F. H. Wines, chairman, "Laws of Settlement and the Right to Public Relief": Report of Committee, *Proceedings, NCCC: 1898*, p. 230.

29. Frederic Almy, "Public Pensions to Widows: Experiences and Observations Which Lead Me to Oppose Such a Law," *Proceedings, NCCC: 1912*, p. 485.

30. Max Senior, discussion, *Proceedings, NCCC: 1912*, p. 492.

31. Mary E. Richmond, " 'Pensions' and the Social Worker," *The Survey*, Feb. 15, 1913; also *The Long View*, eds. Joanna C. Colcord and Ruth Z. S. Mann, Russell Sage Foundation, New York, 1930, pp. 346–349.

32. Francis H. McLean, "Effects Upon Private Charity of the Absence of All Public Relief," *Proceedings, NCCC: 1901*, pp. 139–146.

33. Gertrude Vaile, "Contributions to Public Welfare," *The Family*, Vol. XXVII, No. 1 (1946), p. 32.

34. *Ibid.*, p. 33.

35. Frederic Almy, "The Relationships of Public and Private Charities," *Proceedings, NCCC: 1916*, p. 305.

V. A National Association

THE FIRST CHARITY ORGANIZATION society in the United States was hardly more than under way when the suggestion was made that there ought to be similar societies in every city and that these societies should be linked together in a national or even an international organization. Such a plan would carry out the idea expressed by S. Humphreys Gurteen in his *Handbook of Charity Organization* (1882), as follows: "By an interchange of information with regard to the most successful methods of helping the poor, or of reforming abuses, the experience of one country may be of benefit to all." [1]

Similar ideas were voiced repeatedly by the Committee on the Organization of Charity, which was appointed by the National Conference of Charities and Correction in 1879 and continued for over twenty years, under different titles and with changing membership. This Committee made yearly reports on the developments in the charity organization field, based on analysis of replies to questionnaires sent to the local societies in advance of the meetings. Some of the early committee reports, notably those of 1881 and 1893, were elaborate, although a few of the societies failed to answer or ignored important questions. In 1883, the Committee felt that "as these societies increase it would seem to be desirable that some means be taken to secure a unity of object and to effect exchanges of experience, and the suggestion has been made that a national organization of these societies be perfected." There were only twenty-eight societies at that time, but the idea of charity organization was being enthusiastically embraced by many who had only superficial knowledge of its principles and methods, and, as a result, mortality among the new agencies was high.

In 1887 the Committee apparently had high hopes for the "Council of Charity Officers," a purely voluntary body, composed of the paid officers of the several charity organization societies of the country, which had undertaken the following experiments:

> A central registration, at Buffalo, N. Y., of all travelling mendicants and impostors, based upon reports from all affiliated societies in the United States. [This was one of many attempts to control the vagrants who drifted aimlessly from city to city.]
> The preparation of a telegraphic code for charitable inquiries. [That is, to get information about an applicant who might have been known in another community. This was later developed in connection with the Transportation Agreement. See p. 30.]
> The compilation of a primer of organized charity for educational use at new centres.
> A plan to secure uniform information concerning methods and results from all kindred societies, as a basis for intelligent action upon the social problems which confront them.
> An effort to introduce the teaching of Charity Organization principles and methods into high schools, colleges, and seminaries.[2]

There is no further mention of the "Council of Charity Officers" in the Committee's reports but a statistical card was prepared by the Committee and printed by the National Conference in 1889. The card had headings for the classification of applicants according to social state, ages, nationality, and so on. Statistics were sought for the purpose of "eliciting the causes of pauperism and exhibiting the results of various methods of dealing with it,"[3] thus offering a basis for reform. Copies of the forms developed were sent to the International Congress of Charities, Correction, and Philanthropy held in Paris in 1889 and received high commendation.

At the National Conferences in 1890 and 1891 the Committee members again raised the question of forming a national organization. They made such statements as: "The societies should organize some systematic method of encouraging the creation of societies in communities where they do not now exist, and of assisting those societies which need help in one way or another."[4] And: "It seems of great importance that . . . co-operation and exchange of information among Charity Organization and kindred societies . . . be inaugurated, for there is a sense of isolation among the smaller societies."[5]

For the next six years the idea was not mentioned in the Committee reports but it was probably not out of mind because in 1897 there was a vigorous proposal: "It has seemed to many of the committee that the time is ripe for an organized effort to plant the approved modern methods of charitable administration, public, private, and personal, throughout the entire country. Such a missionary movement should be pushed by an organized executive force dedicated to that purpose." [6] Prior to this recommendation the Committee, in true charity organization style, had sought and received the approval of fifty of the leading societies, but in spite of this support the proposal was referred to a special committee. And in 1898 this special committee recommended another committee to plan and raise funds for a program to establish and extend "intelligent methods of organization and administration of charities." [7] There the matter rested for seven years.

The Field Department of *Charities*

In 1905, during the sessions of the National Conference of Charities and Correction at Portland, Oregon, the general secretaries of several of the larger charity organization societies throughout the country discussed the possibility of an exchange of financial circulars, reports, letters, appeals, plans, and the like, so that schemes worked up in one city and producing results could be utilized by executive officers in other cities. Such a plan was carried on formerly through the co-operation of several of the societies, but fell into disuse because of changes in personnel and the fact that there was no one person on whom responsibility centered. The suggestion was made that the plan be taken over by the periodical *Charities.** Each society would share in the expense and would send every month to the *Charities* office sufficient copies of each leaflet, report, and so on it issued, these to be distributed from the *Charities* office to the twelve to fifteen agencies co-operating.

---

* *Charities* was started by the New York Charity Organization Society in the 1890's and became a national journal. In 1905 it was merged with *The Commons,* a Chicago publication, and became known as *Charities and The Commons.* Two other journals, *Lend a Hand,* published in Boston, and *Jewish Charity,* New York, also were merged with *Charities.* In 1909 *Charities and The Commons* became *The Survey.*

A memo written by Paul U. Kellogg, editor of *Charities,* on October 26, 1905, described the plan:

> At the first meeting of *Charities* Publication Committee early this month, it was decided that one of the most definite services it could render would be to assist in extending the organization of philanthropy to cities in which societies have not yet been formed. Last year several such societies were organized in such widely separated quarters as Portland, Maine, Atlanta, Georgia, and the far Southwest. The movement, however, has been helter skelter and there has been no central agency which could supply leaflets and information, or which could take up with leading citizens the matter of organizing in their towns. It was felt that this extension work is one in which the stronger societies would be willing to co-operate as a part of their educational work and as a duty toward the movement in general.
>
> These two plans have been combined in a new department under *Charities* Publication Committee of which Miss Mary E. Richmond of Philadelphia has consented to take charge. The routine work will be carried forward in *Charities* office and Miss Richmond will have general editorial supervision and will decide upon leaflets and reprints for the purpose of philanthropic extension. The work of the department may be summarized as follows:
>
> 1. Issue of pamphlets, reprints, etc., for distribution in cities in which movements are on foot, or can be developed, to organize charities.
>
> 2. Exchange service of reports, circular letters, appeals, among societies in the larger cities.
>
> Constituent societies are asked to subscribe $30 a year ($2.50 per month) to meet the expense. This will leave a margin above the outlay for clerical work and postage sufficient to make a start in the issue of educational matter. Payment one-half in advance is necessary in order that the work may be undertaken at once.

To carry forward this plan the Field Department of *Charities* (changed later that year to *Charities and The Commons*) was established, with an Exchange Branch. A correspondence service was added to advise on the starting of new societies and the further development of those under way. Francis H. McLean, who had suggested the idea, was given the post of associate editor and was in charge of the correspondence, while continuing as superintendent of the Brooklyn society. As part of his work, he wrote a much-needed pamphlet, *The Formation of Charity Organization Societies in Smaller Cities,*[8] the first of several on this subject.*

---

* Other pamphlets issued by the Field Department, as listed in 1909, included: *The Broadening Sphere of Organized Charity* by Robert W. deForest; *First Principles in the Relief of Distress* by Mary E. Richmond; *Organization in Smaller Cities* by Alexander Johnson; *The Dominant Note of Modern Philanthropy* by Edward T. Devine.

At a meeting in 1907 of the subscribing members of the Exchange Branch, then numbering sixteen, Mr. McLean reported that during the preceding year forty-five cities had written for literature and advice. "We seek," he wrote to Miss Richmond, "to obtain as clear and definite a picture as possible of the local situation, realizing that there are local elements which must always be taken into account before giving advice."

The use that had been made of the correspondence service convinced many of the executives that it should be continued and that additional service should be provided. Paul Kellogg had already written Miss Richmond that the Field Department, which was the first concerted movement for the extension of organized charity, ought to employ a full-time person. He felt that such a service had been needed for at least ten years and might well be financed by the societies themselves. The suggestion was greeted with enthusiasm and with promises of financial support. The plan involved more than the enlargement of the Exchange Branch and the Field Department. In a letter to Edward T. Devine, executive of the New York Charity Organization Society, Miss Richmond wrote on July 2, 1907: "There is a growing desire for a national movement to extend charity organization in new communities and to raise its methods to an ever higher standard in the old ones. The societies wish to help in such a movement and naturally wish to feel that it is their movement."

The new undertaking was outlined at the Exchange Branch meetings at the National Conference in Minneapolis in 1907. Mr. McLean agreed to serve as field secretary under a Field Department Committee with Miss Richmond as chairman, and the Exchange Branch became a separate project, henceforth electing its own executive committee. The Field Department, however, continued to have a close relationship with the societies in the Exchange Branch and with the informal conferences of charity organization secretaries held each year at the National Conference, and continued to be guided by their advice and suggestions. The $7,500 needed to cover the salary of the field secretary and other expenses of the new service came from the newly formed Russell Sage Foundation, not, as had first been planned, from the societies.

During the next two years the Field Department laid a sound

foundation for the soon-to-be-born national association and set the pattern for many of the activities and methods which would be part of future developments. The work of the two field secretaries (Margaret F. Byington joined the staff in January, 1909) was described by Miss Richmond in the introduction to Mr. McLean's pamphlet on organizing societies in smaller cities, mentioned above:

> They studied local conditions in city after city, submitting to each a suggested form of organization or reorganization and serving each, so far as possible, in working the proposed plan out. No visit was paid without an invitation from those locally interested but many invitations were forthcoming and the results achieved were practical and far-reaching.

In addition to field visits and correspondence, the Department, with the help of one office worker, put out a monthly bulletin—mimeographed the first year, printed the second—which dealt with many of the problems facing the societies. An issue of the Field Department *Bulletin* in 1908 gave a summary and analysis of salary scales, hours of work, vacation periods, and so on, based on material from forty-eight societies. Mr. McLean found some of the salaries shockingly inadequate and did not hesitate to urge upward revisions. He commented, "The question is whether the person who has the immensely important *social* duty of supervising the destiny of families is not worth a pretty good salary."

The Department published a directory of charity organization societies, prepared exhibits of forms, case records, and publications for display at the National Conference (the first at Richmond in 1908), mimeographed or printed case records for teaching purposes, and arranged inter-city meetings of societies near some conveniently located centers. On the recommendation of the Department, the Russell Sage Foundation financed a special training district in the New York Charity Organization Society where students from the New York School of Philanthropy could be placed for supervised practice. It was in this period that the Department participated in the first broadly based community survey in this country, that of Pittsburgh. Mr. McLean's section was a study of the "Charities of Pittsburgh," the report of which appeared in *Charities and The Commons* (1909), and Miss Byington made a study published by the Russell Sage Foundation in 1910 under the title *Homestead*.[9]

In the conduct of many of its activities the Field Department
followed a familiar charity organization pattern in its use of committees not only for general oversight of the work but for special
projects as well. There were committees to develop case record
forms, to prepare exhibits for state and national conferences, to read
and comment on case records sent in by agencies, to develop "forwarding centers," * and others appointed as the need arose. These
committees gave a number of board and staff members of local
societies a wide acquaintance with some of the problems of charity
organization societies and with what was being done to meet them,
and thereby strengthened the interest in a national organization. By
the time of the National Conference meetings at Buffalo in June,
1909, this interest was sufficiently widespread to warrant serious
consideration of next steps. A plan for a national organization,
drafted by Mr. McLean after consultation with the leading charity
organization secretaries, was presented to the Exchange Branch,
which was, at that time, the only formally organized group in the
charity organization movement. The Exchange Branch elected
a committee to work on plans to create a national organization and
to report at a meeting of the Branch to be held at the National
Conference in St. Louis the following year. Frederic Almy, executive of the Buffalo society, was elected chairman.

Working Toward a National Organization

In the meantime the Russell Sage Foundation, which had financed
the Field Department for two years, felt that the needs of the local
societies called for an extension of the work and proposed that the
Department be reorganized as the Charity Organization Department of the Foundation. Mary Richmond, who had been the unpaid chairman and editor of the Field Department of *Charities and
The Commons,* agreed to serve as director on condition that the plan
in no way interfere with the societies' forming their own association.
The new department, with Francis H. McLean and Margaret F.

---

* A "forwarding center," usually one in each state, undertook to develop
correspondents in communities where there was no charity organization society
and to forward to these correspondents requests for information that would
help in planning for a family known to the inquiring agency.

Byington joining the staff, started its work October 1, 1909, and for the next two years carried on the program begun under *Charities and The Commons,* plus related activities in social work education and publications.

Meanwhile the local charity organization societies worked toward the completion of plans for a national association which had been outlined at Buffalo. The invitation to the 1910 meeting, sent by the organizing committee to family societies, said it was "most essential at this time to develop a parallel national democratic movement which shall undertake on an increasingly large scale the work of charity organization extension"; otherwise the very success of the Charity Organization Department might delay indefinitely the possibility of an association belonging to the societies.

The organizing committee elected by the Exchange Branch proceeded slowly and carefully, with due attention to different points of view. It held a number of meetings and consulted not only with the members of the Exchange Branch but with other charity organization secretaries as well. At St. Louis in 1910 the committee recommended the temporary organization of a national association, with formal action to be postponed for a year while a committee carried on the work of interpretation and prepared a tentative constitution, bylaws, program, and budget, to be sent to local societies three months prior to the National Conference sessions in Boston in 1911.

The Association Is Founded

The final step was taken on June 8, 1911, and at long last the National Association of Societies for Organizing Charity was launched.* The constitution provided for the full participation of the societies in all affairs of the Association, in the selection of the Board of Directors (at that time called the Executive Committee)

---

* In 1912 "American" was substituted for the word "National" in the name so as to include Canadian agencies. In 1917 the name was shortened to American Association for Organizing Charity. In 1919 it was changed to American Association for Organizing Family Social Work, in 1930 to Family Welfare Association of America, and in 1946 to its present form, Family Service Association of America. For convenience, "the Association" will be used hereafter.

to be drawn from boards and staffs of local agencies, and in the planning of activities. Financial support was to come from membership dues and from contributions raised by the societies. The Russell Sage Foundation had given the venture its endorsement but had made clear its feeling that the Foundation should not be asked for financial help. True to charity organization tradition the societies agreed that "charity organization societies ought not to wish to be pauperized." This corresponded to the hope Miss Richmond had expressed two years earlier in a Charity Organization *Bulletin* "that, should a national agency be launched [as well as the Charity Organization Department] the two agencies created to advance the charity organization cause would be mutually helpful but quite independent of one another, both financially and in management."

At a second meeting, held on June 14, 1911, the business of organization was completed with the election of a board, the approval of a budget of $10,000 for the coming year, and the appointment of a finance committee. The Charity Organization *Bulletin* reported: "At this point somebody proposed that right then and there a test be made of the amount of money that could be furnished by the cities represented in the meeting. Promptly Miss Higgins said $1,000 from Boston and then the enthusiasm broke loose." One city after another pledged support until a total of more than $6,000 had been reached. The fifty-nine agencies represented at these first two meetings came from twenty-five states and the District of Columbia, some from the West and the South, but the majority from cities east of the Mississippi and north of the Potomac.*

"It is well within the truth," wrote Miss Richmond in 1909, "to say that without Mr. McLean's large vision of possibilities then [1906] and without his working out in most careful detail of practical plans since, there would be no Charity Organization Department today."

However well deserved the tribute, Mr. McLean always saw himself as part of a team. It was due not only to him but to Miss Richmond, and to others in the leading charity organization socie-

---

* The actual number of agencies that indicated—some by correspondence—their desire to affiliate was sixty-two. (See Appendix, pp. 177–179.)

ties as well, that the Field Department of *Charities and The Commons* laid the foundations for both the Charity Organization Department and the national organization. During the five years between 1906 when the correspondence service was started and 1911 when the Association was formed, Mr. McLean and those who worked with him had acquired a fund of information about the problems of agencies and communities and how to deal with them. The agencies, on their part, had learned the value of having a national field service at their command and were beginning to have a sense of solidarity. These were definite assets for the Association and Mr. McLean was obviously the person to continue the developments in whose beginnings he had played so large a part. In July, 1911, he was appointed general secretary by unanimous vote of the Board.

One of the first jobs to demand attention was that of dividing between the Association and the Charity Organization Department the responsibilities that had been carried by the latter during the two previous years. A joint committee had worked out a plan which was presented to the Association Board at its first meeting, and which was accepted there and also by the Department. The chief purpose of the Association, as given in its constitution, was "to promote the extension, co-operation, and standardization of such societies for organizing charity in this country." It was in line with this purpose that the Association accepted responsibility for "organizing and reorganizing charity organization societies and promoting their co-operative development" by field visits, correspondence, and other appropriate methods.

The Charity Organization Department undertook, as stated in its *Bulletin,* to "study, teach, and publish in the charity organization field, bounding that field broadly to include the better coordination of all social service." The Department assumed responsibility for the Transportation Agreement (see p. 30) and served as agent for the Exchange Branch until that project was terminated in 1925.

In general, the job of the Association was thought of as extensive, that of the Department as intensive, but some activities were to be shared, such as teaching, recruiting of personnel, further development of community social surveys, and so on. The plan was flexible and subject to revision as the needs of the field changed and as the Association might be able to undertake additional activities.

The Association, unlike the Department, was a co-operative enterprise to be maintained and controlled by its members. It had been created with the expectation, expressed by Edward T. Devine in the *Bulletin,* that it would "first standardize the constituent members' methods and principles and then raise them; lend encouragement and give the bond of unity hitherto lacking." It would give assistance in starting new societies, in reshaping old ones, and would serve as a channel of communication in the development of the movement. At the time the Association was started, nearly two hundred so-called charity organization societies were known to be in existence, but, of these, fewer than one-third were doing the kind of work the name implied.

The constitution did not specify how the Association's program was to be carried out but field service and committee activities, which had previously been under the Field Department of *Charities and The Commons,* were accepted as basic. Field service was recognized as the means not only by which charity organization would be extended but by which all other services would be channeled to the membership and the needs of the membership conveyed to the national body. As initiated under the Field Department and continued by the Association, field service followed the traditional principles of charity organization, beginning with the conviction that each community was different from every other and must develop its own program to meet its peculiar needs. Mr. McLean thought of field service as a form of casework with agencies and communities, analogous to casework with families and individuals—with all that the term implied of individualization, a desire for help, active participation in making and carrying out plans, and self-determination—for the ultimate product had to be the creation of the group concerned, whether it was a family, an agency, or a community.

In the early years much of the field service was concerned with organization or reorganization of charity organization societies, but there were also many requests from established societies for help in problems of personnel, money raising, relations with other agencies, improvement of casework standards, and so on. Through the years these requests continued to increase in number and diversity. Whatever the nature of the request, in order to assure sound development the field worker had to study not only the agency but the community, discover its special characteristics, and interpret and help adapt a variety of experiences to meet the requirements of the local situation.

In the course of getting the basic information about a given community the field worker learned a good deal about the over-all program for family welfare, what was being done to provide needed resources or to correct conditions responsible for the destitution or distress of families over which the families had no control. He had to be prepared to interpret these findings to the local group and to suggest ways in which necessary changes might be brought about. The field worker thus became a community organizer in fact if not in name. At the meeting of the societies in St. Louis in 1910, Mr. McLean described the development of field work:

> There grew up the making of social inquiries, a form of social survey, which means an attempt, through the avenues of readily consulted statistics and reports, personal interviews with experienced local observers and personal observation, at discovering the broad outlines of social development and social need and offering this as a basis or program for future growth.

This type of study, which might be a quick review of a group of social agencies or an extensive survey of social needs and services in many fields, was used extensively during the first fifteen years of the Association. It was superseded by studies limited to the family agencies in a given community or by the more elaborate surveys in which a number of national agencies participated.

Development of Central Councils

The early field studies often revealed a "philanthropic chaos" not unlike that which had inspired the beginnings of charity organization. These studies suggested to Mr. McLean the idea of a separate organization in each community which would take over the traditional function of charity organization in the co-ordination and correlation of charitable agencies. The first central council of social agencies was organized by Mr. McLean in Pittsburgh in 1908.[10] Such a council, he believed, would bring the leaders of all movements into a common federation of interests and would make it possible to plan for the future of the city's social development just as city planning had meant the same careful, sane preparation for municipal development.

The general plan was similar to that of the representative assembly, council, or district committee which charity organization societies had set up for the same purpose, except that the new organization, unlike the charity organization society, would have a direct administrative responsibility only in matters that concerned its own internal affairs. The central councils eventually took over various activities that charity organization had initiated, such as the registration bureau, charities directory, charities endorsement, and became the medium for joint action in correcting adverse social conditions. The charity organization society, as a responsible member of a council, did not, however, give up its interest in community action.

In Chicago, for instance, "The Council of Social Agencies, formed in 1914, assumed functions of leadership in community planning of social work formerly carried by the United Charities, but the [latter] continued to be active in movements for social betterment." [11] Later Mr. McLean expressed his conviction that the family society should be the center of the family casework of a city but "It could not be one of the important social agencies and at the same time be an informal federation of all," as demonstrated by the efforts of charity organization societies to be both. "A really strong family agency can present matters for consideration more frequently than when it had to organize each project itself." [12]

Field Service and Membership

In its First Annual Report, for 1911, the Association noted that the demands for field service, as had been anticipated, "soon exceeded all present resources for such work," involving as it did visits to communities widely scattered geographically (the fifty-one societies visited the first year were located in twenty-one states and Canada) and correspondence which had to be handled on an individual basis. Follow-up work either by personal visits or correspondence

88

was imperative because "even when a group is apparently started along the right road of organization, before one knows it they have picked up a queer idea from somewhere and the work has to be done all over again."

Fortunately the Association was, from its inception, seen as a co-operative enterprise entailing the participation of its constituency in all its activities. Field service was no exception, and it was accepted as a matter of course that the executives of some of the well-established agencies would make field visits when the need arose as they had done before the Association was started. Such volunteer help was necessary to relieve the field staff, which was always limited in number—until 1919 there were never more than three workers, often only one or two—but in addition the executive and the local agency as well as the Association benefited by knowledge of the field and its problems gained by actual contact with other communities. A less direct type of participation was through inter-city conferences, limited to representatives of family societies in a given area. These were usually initiated but not controlled by the field worker, and they focused discussion on problems common to the group, promoted acquaintance among the agencies, and developed a common understanding of methods and principles. A few of these inter-city conferences acted as informal advisory committees to the Association on needs and problems of an area.

Closely integrated with the field service was the Membership Committee. When the Association was started, the societies that had associated themselves in a national body were faced with the immediate necessity of determining the basis on which other societies might be admitted to the group without lowering the level of competence necessary to carry the responsibilities assigned to the constituency by the constitution. To meet this need the first constitution listed five requirements for affiliation and provided for a committee, drawn from the member societies, to examine and act on applications. All actions of this committee were subject to the approval of the Association Board and of the annual meeting, thus assuring full participation of the membership in shaping the character of their national body.

Four requirements were given in the first constitution:

1. A paid agent or secretary on full time; but this provision does not apply to cities with a population of less than 10,000.

2. Individual records and exchange of information.

3. Signing of rules governing the issuance of transportation by charitable societies and public officials as promulgated by National Conference of Charities and Correction.*

4. An agreement to answer inquiries sent to it by societies for organizing charity in other cities.

These requirements were recognized as minimum; it was important that they be suited to both large and small societies, not lag too far behind the most advanced or be too far ahead of those struggling to keep up. The Membership Committee was authorized to "commend higher standards when it seemed desirable." The first amendments were adopted in 1916: "The directorate must be elected by their own membership which shall be open to all persons in the community without regard to their affiliation with any other organization," and "The society shall have a paid secretary who has had at least one year's training in a charity organization society of good standards or any agency having similar methods and standards of case work. This secretary, except in cities of less than 10,000, is to be employed full time." The changes and additions in the requirements since 1916 have reflected the steady development in the work of the societies, with increasing emphasis on such factors as the content of casework, qualified staff, dynamic leadership of both board and staff, concern about social conditions affecting family

---

* At the meeting of the National Conference of Charities and Correction in 1902 the Committee on Needy Families in Their Homes (formerly Committee on Organization of Charities) appointed a committee to draft rules similar to those in use by the Hebrew Charities to control the pernicious practice of "passing on" applicants for aid, with no assurance that transportation to another community would benefit the individual, and to develop a telegraphic code. This committee made its report in 1903, and thereafter for many years both public and private agencies were urged to sign this Transportation Agreement. The rules also offered an effective means for educating the public, especially city officials and the railroads, to the "passing-on" evil. From 1907 to 1909 the Field Department of *Charities and The Commons* acted for the National Conference in promulgating these rules and getting signers; in 1909 the Charity Organization Department of Russell Sage Foundation accepted the responsibility and carried it until 1922, when a committee of representatives from national agencies took over. From 1911 to 1933, signing the Transportation Agreement was a requirement for membership in the Association and for inclusion in the yearly directory of agencies.

life, and active participation in the affairs of the Association. The Membership Committee also adopted provisos that would help guarantee a stable constituency; for example, application for membership must come from the board of a society and only after at least one year of successful operation.

With requirements such as these, membership increased slowly. By 1912 the number of member societies totaled 84; in 1916 the total reached 155; in 1918 there were 170 in spite of losses due to the depression of 1914–15, to the war, and to the inability of agencies to get or keep workers because of the demands for personnel by the Red Cross and other war-connected agencies. At first only non-sectarian, privately supported charity organization or family social work societies were admitted to membership. Later, eligibility was extended to others doing family social work: in 1921 to public departments, in 1928 to units of Mothers Assistance Funds, in 1929 to Jewish agencies, and in 1930 to Catholic agencies. Eventually membership became meaningful as a society recognized that its own work was strengthened when it could ally itself with other like-minded societies, as the Association executive, David H. Holbrook, said in 1923, "in a united program for the protection of family life"—a program to be focused and facilitated through the Association.

Other Association Committees

The Membership Committee was one of a group of committees—administrative, finance, annual meeting, and so on—which enabled the membership to share in the management and to determine the policies of the Association. Other committees, appointed as the need arose, focused the thinking of representative groups on problems of the field as revealed through field visits and other contacts, and their reports, like those of the Membership Committee, were subject to the approval of the board and of the constituency.

The first of these committees was appointed at the Annual Meeting in 1912 at the request of a number of the societies which felt that the "homeless man" situation was one of the most difficult with which they were dealing and wanted to know if it would be possible to work out a program that would lessen wandering. Here was a perennial problem that had been tackled many times before and since charity organization had started, but since there was no doubt as to its urgency, the Association appointed a Committee on the Homeless. This Committee, continued over a number of years with different titles and changing personnel, made various studies, made suggestions for local programs and for inter-city and inter-state control of the drifting population, and finally helped to organize, and then merged with, a committee representing several national agencies. There was, from the first, agreement that the problem was national in scope and called for planning on a national scale. This first committee had significance less for what it accomplished, though that was noteworthy, than for the procedures it instituted for gathering factual material from the agencies which set a pattern for later committees.

The committee system was developed slowly in response to established need. In the years between 1912 and 1918 only a few matters were assigned to committees for study—statistics, "inflow of new workers" (recruiting), publicity, salary schedules—all of them problems of long-time concern to local agencies. This whole period was one of great pressures and of rapid developments in social work as in human affairs in general. The economic depression of 1914–15, the first world war with its disruption of family life, the need for social caseworkers in the Red Cross Home Service, and the organization of specialized agencies to carry some of the responsibilities hitherto borne by family societies vitally affected the programs and resources of the member societies, which were now looking to the Association for wider and more frequent help.

In view of the over-all situation it was not surprising that the Annual Meeting of the membership in 1918 made the following recommendation:

> There should be a study made as to what point we have reached and what should be the future scope and plan of our societies in main essentials. Certainly no longer can the need or apparent need for relief be accepted as indicating anything with reference to the kinds of families with which our societies are working when heavy percentages of our clients come to us with no relief problems. Disorganized family life would more nearly describe it. So do we need definite criteria as to where our responsibilities end and those of specialized agencies begin. For what parts of the community program should we be responsible?

In this period of searching we need a nation-wide definition of work and responsibilities and inter-relations with recognition of the many necessary local variations.

These questions called for thoughtful consideration by a group representing both boards and staffs of the member agencies and a Committee on Future Scope and Policy was appointed, to report at the next annual meeting.

References

1. S. Humphreys Gurteen, *A Handbook of Charity Organization*, published by the author, Buffalo, 1882, p. 207.
2. Charles D. Kellogg, chairman, "Organization of Charities": Report of the Committee on the Organization of Charities, *Proceedings of the National Conference of Charities and Correction: 1887*, p. 128.
3. Charles D. Kellogg, chairman, "Charity Organization in the United States": Report of the Committee on History of Charity Organization, *Proceedings, NCCC: 1893*, p. 77.
4. Nathaniel S. Rosenau, chairman, "Charity Organization": Report of the Committee on Charity Organization, *Proceedings, NCCC: 1890*, p. 31.
5. Hannah M. Todd, chairman, "Charity Organization": Report of the Committee on Organization of Charities, *Proceedings, NCCC: 1891*, p. 118.
6. Alfred O. Crozier, chairman, "Organization of Charity": Report of the Committee on Organization of Charity, *Proceedings, NCCC: 1897* (special volume, Section on Organization of Charities), p. 7.
7. Charles R. Henderson, Report of Special Committee, *Proceedings, NCCC: 1898*, p. 483.
8. Francis H. McLean, *The Formation of Charity Organization Societies in Smaller Cities*, Russell Sage Foundation, New York, 1910.
9. Margaret F. Byington, *Homestead: The Households of a Mill Town*, Russell Sage Foundation, New York, 1910.
10. Francis H. McLean, *The Central Council of Social Agencies*, American Association for Organizing Family Social Work, New York, 1920. See also: "Central Councils," *The Family*, Vol. XXVI, No. 1 (1946), pp. 23–25.
11. Florence Nesbitt, *The Family Service Bureau, United Charities of Chicago*, United Charities of Chicago, 1941, pp. 10–11.
12. Francis H. McLean, *The Family Society*, American Association for Organizing Family Social Work, New York, 1927, p. 118.

VI. A New Era

WITH THE ADOPTION of the Report of the Committee on Future Scope and Policy at the Association's 1919 Annual Meeting, the charity organization movement, to quote Mary E. Richmond, "took on new life with a new declaration of principles and a new name dedicating the movement to the promotion of family welfare." [1]

The majority of the Committee's recommendations were focused on the family. Casework service to families was considered the primary responsibility of the societies; it would include the interpretation of casework findings in order to promote conditions that would protect and strengthen family life, such as reforms in marriage laws and their administration, and higher wages and better working conditions. Division of work with other agencies, including those under public auspices, was to be based on what was best for the family. Also considered basic to the promotion of normal family life was a study of factors that make for the preservation and enrichment of the home. Other recommendations—the use of volunteers, the development of more and better facilities for training volunteers and staff, and the recognition of the individuality of communities—reaffirmed traditional principles of charity organization.

The Committee took cognizance of the changed attitudes about relief giving since the days when the majority of the societies believed, as Mary E. Richmond had said in 1890, that "as soon as

94

the charity organization society becomes a relief-giving society also, it signs its own death-warrant."[2] In 1918 Miss Richmond stated that not only did most of the societies have their own funds for relief, but they had allowed themselves "to become gradually the general relief pocket of the whole community,"[3] including other agencies. The Committee recommended that "while . . . each society must work out the problem according to its individual situation, the general principles should be recognized that we are not forced by the essential nature of our work to monopolize the field where relief is concerned," and further "that member societies consider investigation and treatment as inseparable . . . that, wherever it is feasible, other agencies in the field be encouraged to undertake the whole treatment needed by families in which they are interested, even where this needed treatment includes the giving of relief."[4] Ten years later these admonitions were to be repeated by the Milford Conference.

The idea of the family as the unit of service was not new. In 1890 Zilpha D. Smith had said:

> We of the Charity Organization Societies come to the National Conference as few other members do, and owe it a peculiar debt. Most of you deal with poor persons or defective or delinquent persons as *individuals,* removed from family relations. We deal with the *family* as a whole, usually working to keep it together, but sometimes helping to break it up into units, and to place them in your care. Not a subject is treated in the Conference that it is not necessary we should know about some time in the course of the year's work, in order to use wisely the special agencies about us. We cannot afford to miss a single session of the whole week. We are general practitioners; and we have much to learn from you, the specialists.[5]

When the societies set up the national organization in 1911 they had again emphasized their primary interest in the family. At that first meeting in Boston in 1911, Edward T. Devine, executive of the New York Charity Organization Society, had said, "Family rehabilitation is but an expression of an idea which has always been present but the new expression of it corresponds to a very desirable change of emphasis."

Now, in 1919, the Committee on Future Scope and Policy suggested that the societies underline their interest in the family by calling themselves family social work, instead of charity organization, societies. Charity organization had become so identified with economic help that it stood in the way of the societies' giving needed services to those not economically dependent.

In line with the 1919 report it was voted to change the name of the national organization from American Association for Organizing Charity to American Association for Organizing Family Social Work and to urge local agencies to use the words "family social work" if and when they adopted new titles. The purpose of the Association was rephrased to conform to its new title—"to promote the extension and development of family social work in the United States and Canada."

The tempo and scope of activities outlined by the Committee on Future Scope and Policy called for expansion and extension of the facilities of the national organization. The 1919 Annual Meeting therefore voted to increase the field staff from two to five, with Mr. McLean as field director, and to set up an executive department with a director and an associate to be responsible for publicity, finances, committee activities, publications—including a monthly periodical—and informational material about experiments and experiences of the entire field. The cost of this expansion was to be met in part by a grant from the Russell Sage Foundation, in part by contributions from the membership, which was expected eventually to carry the entire expense.

Without waiting to fill all the positions authorized at the Annual Meeting, the Association moved ahead immediately on the new program. In 1920 David H. Holbrook was named as the director of the new executive department. During 1919–20 the field staff visited three times as many agencies as in the previous year, and it must be remembered that field service included much more than visiting and advising with local societies; its staff organized intercity and regional meetings, attended state conferences, and advised on the organization of central councils of social agencies.

New Publications

In February, 1920, the new executive department launched an informal *News Letter,* devoted primarily to news of the membership and of the national organization. In March, 1920, the Association began publication of a monthly journal, *The Family* (now *Social*

Casework). Although the *Bulletin* and other publications of the Charity Organization Department of the Russell Sage Foundation had been devoted to the interests of family social work, the societies for some years had discussed the possibility of a magazine of their own. The Charity Organization Department discontinued the *Bulletin* in 1918 in order to leave the way open for the new venture, which Miss Richmond supported and encouraged. From the outset, *The Family* indicated its intention to continue the policy of the *Bulletin* of presenting "material hammered out of experience" and both directly and indirectly invited board members, volunteers, and staff to write about what they were seeing and doing and thinking. The new journal was designed primarily for family social workers but was in no way limited to them either in subject matter or circulation and its advisory committee included representatives from medical social work and child welfare as well as from the family field.

It was a good time to open up opportunities for professional writing. *Social Diagnosis* had given caseworkers a new interest in the study of their own jobs and this interest was further stimulated by Mary E. Richmond's next book, *What Is Social Case Work?*,[6] with its discussion of treatment processes. Here was a subject about which caseworkers knew more than anyone else and the very existence of *The Family* was an indirect invitation to give expression to that knowledge. There were more direct invitations also: Porter R. Lee, director of the New York School of Social Work, wrote in an early issue:

> We must find our way beyond the case records into the thinking and experience of case workers themselves. This is a process in which no one can help us; this mine must be worked by our own efforts. I suggest, as a practice promising greater improvement in the quality of our case work than would follow from any other, the regular analysis by case workers themselves of the factors which have entered into their conspicuous successes and failures in human leadership.[7]

The advisory committee and the editors wanted not only articles about casework but also material dealing with subjects that were part of the everyday experience of family societies and other casework agencies—the work of the board as well as the staff, of volunteers and committees, and reports of community needs as revealed

97

by casework contacts with individuals and families. They hoped to make the journal a "workshop of ideas."

Further encouragement to scrutinize the casework job and what family societies were doing in other areas came from the Committee on Content of Family Social Work, appointed by the Association in 1921 to study the content of family social work and to indicate the technical requirements as well as the ends being sought by the family societies. The Committee studied case records and other material from agencies all over the country and enlisted the interest of staff groups and of a seminar at the New York School of Social Work in making similar studies. The Committee's report (1926) was, therefore, a composite of material from many sources; it indicated some of the areas where family social work was weak or uneven, as in problems of vocational and industrial adjustment, but found that there was general acceptance of the basic concept that "our purposes must always tie up with the release of our clients' dynamic qualities and their attainment of self-direction," however weak the methodology might be at times.[8]

The Committee realized that its report was in no sense final, that its chief value was in providing an outline of the attainable and desirable in family social work at that time; it recognized that the process of definition must be continuous, growing with the development of family casework and enriched by new discoveries and new concepts of what was possible in the adjustment of human relations.

Organizational Committees

Other committees of the new era were concerned with the operation of family social work from what might be called the organizational angle. A Committee on Salary Schedules had been appointed in 1918 and its report was printed in the first two issues of *The Family*, in March and April, 1920. The Committee—consisting of four family caseworkers, one worker from an employment bureau, and one board member—gave their time over a two-year period to a study of salaries and expenditures of caseworkers in twenty-eight cities. In the tabulation of caseworkers' budgets, the Committee reported that the "chief point which stands out is the utter discrepancy beween salary and expenditure. Many workers, in answer to the query on the questionnaire, 'How long have you been self-supporting?' replied: 'I have never tried to live on my salary.'" The Committee recognized that these conditions were deplorable, unlikely to "create a profession which will attract the best new blood." They urged the larger societies to start a movement for decent salaries which might well be later followed by the smaller agencies.[9]

This study of salaries, with its recommendations, was an important step toward much-needed staff stabilization, increasing the worker's self-respect, and adding dignity to the job. Studies of salaries became a regular activity, and the Association eventually established standards that were useful to other casework agencies as well as to family societies. Other matters relating to personnel—recruiting, training, employment practices, working conditions, personnel standards, and staff development—were taken up in the early 1920's by committees which, with changing titles and personnel, have been continued to the present time.

The recommendation of the Association Board in 1918 that member societies give their support to the development of strong public welfare departments was followed in 1920 by the appointment of a Committee on Relations Between Public and Private Family Agencies. This was in line with the recommendation of the Committee on Future Scope and Policy that family societies should clarify and define their relations with other agencies. The new Committee, with Gertrude Vaile of Denver as chairman, followed the usual procedure of going direct to the agencies for information about existing conditions and suggestions for future plans. From this informal survey the Committee was able to give a picture of current practices, to outline principles and philosophy which had evolved through the years, and to suggest next steps. Even before it completed its final report,[10] the Committee was able to make some practical suggestions; for example, that any legislation or ordinance establishing a public department should provide for an unpaid advisory committee to be administratively responsible for the work, that the commissioner be a trained social worker, and that the rest of the staff be under civil service.

In 1921 the Committee proposed an amendment to the constitution of the Association: "Public Departments doing family social work according to standards equivalent to those required for active membership on the part of private societies may be admitted as annual active members, such membership to be renewable upon yearly review by the membership committee." This amendment was passed at the Annual Meeting of the Association in Milwaukee, June, 1921; the Denver Department was the first to be admitted to membership (1922). The Committee's final recommendations were accepted at the Annual Meeting in Denver in June, 1925. In substance it was agreed that ordinarily both public and private agencies for family social work are needed, independent of each other but with good teamwork between them; any division of responsibility must be worked out locally, preferably through joint committees or conference discussion; casework in the public department is essential and should be encouraged by the board of the private agency; the public agency should assume the heaviest part of the relief burden but the private agency should give relief when indicated in situations where it was giving casework service.

One suggestion—not a recommendation—was that "the private society doing family case work of a high order may extend its services to clients who can pay, even as visiting nurse associations do." The same suggestion had been made earlier and was to be made repeatedly before it was given a trial. The acceptance of the Committee's recommendation on admitting public departments to Association membership was a step in the long-delayed acceptance of an obligation, envisaged nearly thirty years before by the then existing charity organization societies, "to plant the approved modern methods of charitable administration, public, private, and personal, throughout the entire country." [11]

A National Unemployment Crisis

The Committee on Relations Between Public and Private Family Agencies was able to offer practical, though informal, help when the widespread unemployment of 1921–22 precipitated discussions of interagency relations and of how much responsibility the private family society should carry in meeting the needs of the unemployed. In October, 1921, the Association called a meeting of executives and supervisors of family agencies in thirty-one cities to discuss the practicability of various emergency measures, the desirable relations between public and private agencies in such a crisis, and the contribution family social workers might be expected to make to a constructive program for the future. The discussion brought out varying points of view and experiments which, successful or otherwise, were frankly set forth, and many theories which were decidedly divergent. There was no attempt to take a vote on any of the issues or to outline a program for meeting unemployment which would be applicable the country over. There was agreement, however, on a few basic principles: group responsibility was essential in meeting a community crisis and the family society should share in this; no action should be taken in an emergency which would cripple desirable action under normal circumstances, such as a division of work between public and private family agencies that would assign all relief for the unemployed to the public agency. There was complete agreement that the private family societies must scrutinize their casework methods as never before and must interpret the human cost of unemployment to the community. Mary Van Kleeck, of the Russell Sage Foundation, who was a member of the President's Conference on Unemployment, reported that the conference was emphasizing the need to gather statistics, to speed up public works, and to promote local initiative in meeting the unemployment situation.

The Association's first meeting on unemployment was followed by several regional conferences and a biweekly interchange of letters among the societies carried on through the Association office. *The Family* printed a number of articles about local experiments, in addition to two major statements summarizing basic principles and constructive measures that had stood the test of experience. At the Annual Meeting at Providence in 1922 the Association appointed a Committee on Industrial Problems, recommended by the Committee on Future Scope and Policy, to study and advise on industrial problems affecting the casework of family societies and to consider "what stand, if any, we should take as local societies and as a national organization in reducing in the future large-scale unemployment or at least reducing the evil effects therefrom."

Relations Between National Organizations

The Association had early recognized the importance of sound understanding and working relations between national as well as local organizations. Mr. McLean's first tentative plan for the Association (March, 1909) had suggested that "with the establishment of a national committee such committee shall do its part in bringing about a joint conference of all the national committees and associations to plan out any possible line of joint attack in connection with national conditions and the influencing of national legislation." Some such meetings were held in 1909–10 under the auspices of the Charity Organization Department of the Russell Sage Foundation and seven of the national agencies represented at that time exchanged field work itineraries. Later there were occasional informal consultations.

With the growth of both local and national social agencies during and immediately after World War I, the need for some regular interchange of thinking to prevent duplication and to implement joint action was urgent. One practical and immediate step was the appointment of a committee by the Association in 1919 to confer with the American National Red Cross and work out policies to avoid duplication of services and at the same time further the development of family social work in the many communities where the Red Cross had organized Home Service during the war. Beginning in 1920 both the Red Cross and the Association joined an informal group of national agencies concerned with relationships on local and national levels. The efforts of this group resulted, in 1923, in the organization of the National Social Work Council. David H. Holbrook, who was executive director of the Association, served the new organization first as part-time, unpaid secretary, then resigned from the Association in 1925 to become full-time, paid secretary of the Council. (In 1945 the Social Work Council was reorganized as the National Social Welfare Assembly.) In 1921 members of the Association staff participated in launching the American Association of Social Workers, which in 1955 joined with six other professional groups to form the National Association of Social Workers.

Advancing Knowledge and Skills

Beginning in 1921, the Association and other national agencies met together in informal discussions of developments in the casework field. After the group began holding meetings in Milford, Pennsylvania, in 1923, the group became known as the Milford Conference. It had no organized program but sought, through free

102

discussion, to arrive at an understanding of the similarities and differences in types of casework service.* It was early apparent that "practice had developed more rapidly than the contemplation of its significance or the ability to define it." The need for more intensive discussion led to the appointment of a subcommittee † to formulate answers to the following questions: "(1) What can we understand by generic social case work? (2) Assuming competent agencies in the various case work fields, what is a desirable basis for a division of labor in social case work in a local community? (3) What is a competent agency for social case work? (4) What constitutes training for social work?"

The final report expressed this conviction of the committee:

> There is no greater responsibility facing social case work at the present time than the responsibility of organizing continuous research into the concepts, problems and methods of its field. . . . Social case workers cannot leave the responsibility for research to foundations and universities. They must do it themselves and participation by social case workers in such research must be widespread. The results of such studies . . . are needed for the training of case workers . . . for the development of sounder methods of supervision . . . and for the individual social case worker in his own professional development.[12]

In its discussion of training for social work the report emphasized that the leadership of both agencies and schools was needed to establish and maintain standards. "We suggest, therefore, that steps should be taken . . . to establish a permanent commission or council on education for social work. We believe that both apprentice training and training in the schools would be strengthened at the present time if there were some center through which those responsible for administering professional education could receive from the field authoritative and well-developed suggestions as to what the term 'trained social worker' really implies."[13] The com-

---

* Agencies represented were: American Association for Organizing Family Social Work, American Association of Hospital Social Workers, American Association of Psychiatric Social Workers, Child Welfare League of America, International Migration Service, National Association of Travelers Aid Societies, National Committee on Visiting Teachers, and National Probation and Parole Association. The Milford Conference was discontinued in 1934; later the national casework agencies formed the casework council within the National Social Work Council.

† Porter R. Lee, chairman, Harriet E. Anderson, C. C. Carstens, Mary C. Hurlbutt, Margaret E. Rich. At the end of the first year Miss Hurlbutt was replaced by M. Antoinette Cannon; Christine Robb participated in one meeting.

mittee called its report an outline presented "in the hope that it may stimulate, guide and give coherence to the efforts of social workers . . . to study their own professional problems and equipment."

The suggestions of the Milford Conference on training were particularly timely for family social work. In 1925 the 220 member societies of the Association employed some 2,500 workers, and had, in addition, an unestimated number of volunteers. In that same year the Association took over the Institute of Family Social Work (formerly the Charity Organization Institute) which had been conducted by Miss Richmond from 1910 through 1922. (See pp. 51–52.) In 1925 the Institute was led by Frank J. Bruno of the Minneapolis agency and in later years by Betsey Libbey of the Philadelphia agency.

The Association also sponsored a wide variety of short-term projects—a two-week staff discussion in Toronto led by Ruth Hill, a three-week regional group meeting in Kansas City, Missouri, led by Gertrude Vaile, a round table for general secretaries held in Chicago and led by Mr. McLean, and an informational course for volunteers and board members led by Helen Kempton in Springfield, Massachusetts. None of these was thought of as a substitute for graduate school training; rather they were seen as supplemental to graduate work, refresher courses for workers already employed.

All members of the Association staff shared responsibility for vocational counseling of an informal sort and for placement, which had always been an important part of the national program. The staff, as well as the Association's Committee on Training with Anna Kempshall as chairman, maintained close contacts with schools of social work and helped local societies develop plans for staff training. For a brief period the Association had a special resource, the Alice Higgins Lothrop Memorial Scholarship Fund, of which the nucleus was a legacy to the Association from its second president, Mrs. Lothrop. This provided graduate training for a few individuals; in later years fellowship programs were established by a number of local agencies. The Association's books and pamphlets on organization and administration, its journal *The Family,* the annual case record exhibits, and case records for teaching were widely used by both agencies and schools. The Association served as the instrument for discovering and developing material, soliciting articles, and making the results available.

Fiftieth Anniversary

The celebration of the fiftieth anniversary of the founding of the first city-wide charity organization society in the United States was held in Buffalo in 1927. It was the first national conference in the family field and was distinguished by the plan of arranging a series of meetings focused on a single theme. At Miss Richmond's suggestion, the program, instead of recapitulating the history of family social work during the previous half-century, was devoted to a series of papers on what was happening to family life in America and to informal round tables on topics of current interest to family societies. Only five of the speakers on the regular program were practicing social workers. The others—nine of them—brought the different viewpoints of industry, religion, biology, sociology, economics, and education to bear on the question of what material things and institutions and persons were influencing family life. Taken as a whole, these papers constituted—by their authoritative opinion, specific suggestions, and implied trends of action—a fundamental program for the enrichment of family life in its broadest and deepest sense.[14]

Nine hundred and sixty-one people, most of them board or staff members or volunteers from family societies, attended the three-day meetings. Among them were the Rev. J. C. Pringle, head of the London Charity Organisation Society, and W. E. Hincks, who held a similar position with the Leicester society. In writing about the meetings later, Mr. Pringle spoke of the sense of fellowship that pervaded all the meetings and he expressed the feeling of many who were there that the ovation to Miss Richmond when she rose to read her paper was the high point of the conference, long to be remembered.

The fiftieth anniversary celebration marked, not an end attained, but a fresh beginning. It gave family social work a redefinition of its goals, a new sense of the values in family life, a practical program for enhancing those values through an objective consideration of the social health of the family and its interdependence with community health. The speakers were essentially in agreement that:

> The welfare of the family may well be a touchstone for evaluating the lasting worth of present-day industrial, educational, religious, and other social institutions. If it can be demonstrated that these institu-

tions further a richer and more genuinely successful family life—not as we know family life all about us, but as it might become—then they satisfy one test of their own permanent value.[15]

Indirectly the papers outlined what Miss Richmond described as "a program of next steps which will increase social satisfactions and develop a sounder family life for this generation and the next" [16] —education for family living, counseling in family problems, alertness to the impact of social and industrial conditions on family life, extension of casework services to all families, and study of what makes for success and failure in family life.

References

1. Mary E. Richmond, "A Background for the Art of Helping," *Art of Helping,* Association of Volunteers in Social Service, New York, 1924, p. 25.
2. Mary E. Richmond, *The Long View,* eds. Joanna C. Colcord and Ruth Z. S. Mann, Russell Sage Foundation, New York, 1930, p. 34.
3. *Ibid.,* pp. 461–462.
4. *Report of the Committee on Future Scope and Policy,* American Association for Organizing Charity, New York, 1919, pp. 4, 6.
5. Zilpha D. Smith, discussion on charity organization, *Proceedings of the National Conference on Charities and Correction: 1890,* p. 377.
6. Mary E. Richmond, *What Is Social Case Work?,* Russell Sage Foundation, New York, 1922.
7. Porter R. Lee, "A Study of Social Treatment," *The Family,* Vol. IV, No. 8 (1923), p. 199.
8. *Content of Family Social Work,* Report of a Committee of the American Association for Organizing Family Social Work, Quarterly Bulletin, June, 1926.
9. Committee on Salary Schedules, "Expenditures and Salaries of Case Workers," *The Family,* Vol. I, No. 1, pp. 11–16, and No. 2, pp. 5–8 (1920).
10. *Division of Work Between Public and Private Agencies Dealing with Families in Their Homes,* Report of Committee on Relations with Public Departments, American Association for Organizing Family Social Work, New York, June, 1925.
11. Alfred O. Crozier, chairman, "Organization of Charity": Report of the Committee on Organization of Charity, *Proceedings, NCCC: 1897* (special volume, Section on Organization of Charities), p. 7.
12. *Social Case Work—Generic and Specific,* A Report of the Milford Conference, American Association of Social Workers, New York, 1929, p. 12.
13. *Ibid.,* p. 92.
14. Margaret E. Rich (ed.), *Family Life Today,* Papers presented at fiftieth anniversary of family social work in America, Houghton Mifflin Co., Boston, 1928, p. vi.
15. *Ibid.*
16. Mary E. Richmond, "The Concern of the Community with Marriage," *Family Life Today (supra),* p. 67.

VII. The Depression Years

THE CELEBRATION OF the fiftieth anniversary of American family social work, in 1927, was held on the eve of the widespread industrial depression which overwhelmed the country in the 1930's and brought unprecedented, often disastrous, pressures on family life, not limited to any one social or economic group. In fact the depression had already begun, although it was to become worse in the next year or two. Business conditions improved after the 1921–22 depression but did not fully recover. Charts published by the National Bureau of Economic Research showed a recession in 1923, a mild depression in 1924 followed by a revival.

These fluctuations were reflected in the case loads of family societies but for the most part unemployment was sporadic rather than general. Rising relief expenditures, however, continued to cause uneasiness both locally and nationally and in 1925 the Association appointed a Committee on Material Relief Problems which joined with two other groups—the American Association for Community Organization and the Russell Sage Foundation—in a study of relief expenditures over a ten-year period in thirty-seven representative cities. The results showed that the agencies in these cities had spent three times as much for relief in 1925 as in 1916 and revealed a "uniformity of increase indicating that the problem is not purely local in its significance but arises from conditions more or less common to the whole field." [1] The need for further study was obvious and later the Committee undertook to bring to light some of the trends and changes in practice in relief giving during the ten-year period from 1916 to 1926.

In the meantime case loads in many societies continued to show the number of applications due to lack of work to be higher than normal and the Association enlisted the help of the Statistics Department of the Russell Sage Foundation in making a brief survey of employment conditions in a group of representative cities. The Association *News Letter* reported in 1927 that the returns tended to "confirm our opinion based on employment and other economic indices that, in general, business this winter is considerably poorer than last winter. . . . There seems to be more than seasonal but by no means aggravated depression." [2] Articles in *The Family* spoke of "case workers who have been overwhelmed this winter [1927–28] by widespread problems of unemployment," suggested that unemployment had become a "national calamity," and wondered how long private agencies could continue to deal with the situation.

The Association's Committee on Industrial Problems had been keeping in close touch with local conditions and had prepared material embodying many suggestions, among them some made by the Association during the 1921–22 depression for a year-in year-out community program for stabilizing employment and for meeting an emergency should one arise. This material was presented in 1929, in a pamphlet titled *The Time to Plan Is Now*.[3] The Committee recognized the truth of Mary Richmond's statement in 1921: "Violent fluctuations between times of great scarcity of workers and times of great scarcity of work are due to causes over which the social agencies of the country have little control." [4]

Linton B. Swift, executive secretary of the Association, said in 1929:

> Although it may not be our function to propose any particular remedy for such evils as unemployment, it assuredly is our function to stimulate responsible groups in the community into seeking actively some remedy for community ills which cause distress to the families we serve. There are many possible plans which only need such stimulation toward action. . . . The important thing is the local group thinking which is started. And the plan which will best meet a local situation may originate with local business men.[5]

It was in line with this philosophy that the Committee outlined definite steps to stimulate local group thinking and planning, and urged family societies not to wait until times became worse but to start immediately to organize community committees on unemployment to work toward the adoption of preventive measures and to initiate remedial measures as needed. The Committee expressed these views: centralized planning with decentralized administration was advisable to avoid the massing of unemployed in one place; "made work" or "relief work" was most likely to be helpful only on a highly selective basis, where the job was matched to the capacity of the worker; every effort should be made to stimulate real work and to arrange an equitable distribution of available jobs; some kind of clearing house was essential; public advertising of work relief projects and large centralized funds stimulated applications and attracted non-residents; relief to the individual or family on the basis of need was preferable to breadlines or indiscriminate mass feeding.*

The widespread unemployment and general economic depression following the stock market crash in the fall of 1929 brought a sharp increase in applications for relief and speeded up co-operative planning in local communities. Brief descriptions of what happened in a few cities were given by member societies at the Association's Annual Meeting in June, 1930. Toledo, Ohio, was among the cities hardest hit. The payroll of the largest concern in the city sank from a record high of 26,000 in February, 1929, to a low of 6,000 in November of that year. The change in conditions was reflected in the family society case load as early as October, when the number of applications was 767 as compared with 553 in September; in November it was 1,218; in December, 1,967; in January, 1930, it was 2,727 (as compared with 1,000 the previous year) and in February it rose to 3,459.

---

* Josephine Shaw Lowell felt that the East Side Work Relief Committee in New York City, in 1893–94, had given a maximum amount of help with a minimum of harm largely because "though we had to deal with hundreds we never lumped them and treated them wholesale as a class." Accounts of the attempts of charity organization and family social work to organize relief in unemployment emergencies are available in periodicals and in various National Conference of Social Work *Proceedings*, also in *The Burden of Unemployment*, by Philip Klein,[6] *Cash Relief*, by Joanna C. Colcord,[7] and *Unemployment Relief in Periods of Depression*, by Leah H. Feder.[8]

So enormous an increase in case load called for additional staff and additional funds. The Toledo agency, although financed by the community chest, also administered the city's poor relief, and both chest and city administration responded to the need for funds. That the problem was more difficult than the depression of 1920–22 was shown by comparison of relief expenditures for the six months from November to April in the three years involved: 1920–21, $55,000; 1921–22, $150,000; 1929–30, $219,000. Increases in staff were made so far as workers were available, volunteers were used wherever practicable, and caseworkers were relieved of work that could be transferred to clerical staff. But increase in staff lagged far behind increase in case load; in April, 1930, the staff was 50 per cent larger than in November, 1929, while the case load was 800 per cent larger. Although the Toledo society made no pretense of doing at this time a high grade of social casework—indeed very little casework except in keeping up the morale of clients—it did provide, ungrudgingly and promptly, fairly adequate relief where it was needed. By June, 1930, the society was marshaling community resources in preparation for the coming winter, which seemed likely to be more severe than the last.

A study of employment and unemployment initiated by the Dayton, Ohio, society in the summer of 1929 had clearly indicated the need of a permanent organization for regularization of employment and prevention of unemployment, although it was obvious that there was no immediate remedy for the current situation. A general committee was set up to continue research with four subcommittees: Employment Bureau, Public Works, Fact Finding and Education, and Stabilization. Also, a start was made toward a program for attacking the problem facing the community.

The St. Louis society had been so swamped with applications that, in order to save time of both clients and workers, it had organized an intake department at the central office to take care of all intake instead of handling it in the districts. The Association *News Letter* of October, 1930, reported, "Workers capable of working rapidly and with a minimum of supervision were drafted from the district staffs, ex-workers were called on for temporary service and workers were even loaned by other organizations to form the staff of this new department." Somewhat similar plans were later followed

110

in other cities. The St. Louis society had begun a study of local conditions as early as 1928 and had started a Committee on Industrial Problems but, as Caroline Bedford, a staff member of the society, told the National Conference in 1931, "unfortunately, it [the committee] languished and died. In times of apparent prosperity it seemed impossible to interest a group of business men in the unemployed man and when the depression was upon us there was not time for it." [9] Similar attitudes prevailed in a number of communities where any suggestion of widespread unemployment or of a depression was considered "bad for business."

Cincinnati, Ohio, and Rochester, New York, however, were able to get committees on stabilizing employment under way before the crash. The committee in Cincinnati, the October, 1930, *News Letter* stated, was "not an emergency committee nor an unemployment committee but primarily a committee that deals with the fundamental problems of employment. It will require long periods of study and an accumulation of data with considerable education before any concrete or tangible results are in evidence. Cincinnati employers —for the most part—have willingly co-operated and they can be said really to be seeking light on this important subject." [10]

In Rochester the society focused its 1930 annual meeting on unemployment. A pamphlet entitled *Unemployment,* which included excerpts from *The Time to Plan Is Now,* was distributed at the meeting. To quote the *News Letter* again: "Unemployment—a community problem—needs community action on a continuous basis. The time for planning is when all energy is not of necessity consumed in temporary relief measures. A carefully selected unemployment commission is needed to study this problem, both nationally and locally, and, from the many measures suggested for the mitigation of unemployment, to recommend a plan adaptable to this community." As a result of this meeting the board of the society asked the council of social agencies to form a committee, which was organized in March, 1930, with a membership including leaders in business, civic activities, labor, and social work. "The chief gain to date [October, 1930] is the change of attitude among some of the leading industrialists . . . their doubt and indifference as to the seriousness of the problem have given way to an admission

111

of the serious condition existing and an honest desire to remedy it as far as possible." [11]

Cleveland, like St. Louis, had had a long stretch of high unemployment and the family society had mobilized the strength within the agency and to some extent the neighborhood resources which could be of service. Since Cleveland had no public outdoor relief department, the private agency carried the entire burden of unemployment relief. One district of the society had been particularly successful in working with the employment managers in the district. Weekly meetings were held in which the employment managers were interested enough to attend regularly. They discussed the family situations in detail and secured jobs for almost every man whose case was brought up. In the midst of all the other demands upon staff and board, the Cleveland society was gradually laying the foundations for the establishment of a public department with trained personnel.

Relations with Public Departments

In communities where there were both public and private family agencies there had been some effort prior to the depression to formulate working agreements on division of responsibility, with an increasing tendency to rely on public funds for relief. At the 1929 Annual Meeting the Association's Committee on Future Program, which had been appointed in 1925, recommended some specific next steps in the "sound development of family social work under public auspices": intensive joint study of the problems of public agencies leading toward the development of principles of organization and administration; the use of many channels in interpreting to the community the need for a public agency and adequate standards of work; the development of a public department board or advisory group of well-informed citizens, appointed for overlapping terms and independent of political control as the best safeguard against many of the difficulties faced by public agencies; development of public understanding and support through constant interpretation of the work of the public agency; a program of better co-operation between the public and private agencies, including agreement upon relative areas of responsibility.

112

The public agency members of the Association were particularly helpful in furthering some of these suggested steps and it was at their suggestion that in 1930 the Association appointed a pathfinding committee to explore the nature and possibilities of governmental relief methods. This committee was authorized to include, in addition to a study of family social work under public auspices, a study of old-age and mothers' pensions and other types of relief by categories with or without casework, subsidies to private agencies, and generalized or non-categorical relief administered by government agencies as part of a casework program. The Pathfinding Committee on Governmental Relief Methods was appointed in 1930 with Harry L. Lurie as chairman. Its final report (1932) summed up the basis for the study and recommendations for next steps:

> Public relief has increased during the last few years as never before. The haphazard and unorganized development . . . point to the need for large-scale and systematic study and planning. . . . The committee recommends a concentrated, co-operative, national undertaking extending over a four-year period and embodying the elements of fact-finding, education, and social planning in the field of public relief. . . . Out of such a project it might be possible to develop some consistent social philosophy regarding public welfare and to define some of the issues as to public responsibility, principles of aid, what kind of problems bring clients to an agency and so on.[12]

The Homeless and Transients

The majority of the local plans for division of public and private responsibility were concerned primarily with residents who had some claim on the community; there was little provision for the homeless and transients, not all of them chronic drifters but for whom usually no agency took or wanted to take responsibility. The Association's Committee on the Homeless (see pp. 91–92) saw this as a perennial problem, always aggravated at certain seasons and in periods of depression, calling for co-operation of as large a number of local agencies as possible in formulating some plan for centralized responsibility. The Committee recommended no pattern program but it advised with local groups on the basis of their needs and resources. Particular attention was given to possible plans for intra-state and inter-state control, since transiency was a regional or national, rather than a local, problem.*

For the most part, in 1929–30 programs for the care of homeless and transients were at "sixes and sevens." Many family societies did not accept applications from unattached men or women, whether resident or transient, but joined with other agencies in sponsoring some type of service under either public or private auspices—a central clearing house, a casework interview for every applicant, provision for food and lodging and for transportation if desirable. It was not always possible to convince a planning group that it was essential to use discrimination. As long ago as 1897 Josephine Shaw Lowell wrote, in the *New York Evening Post,* that workers must "treat each one of these unhappy men and women, so far as possible, as individuals, finding out about them and using the knowledge gained to do what is best for him or her." In the beginning of the depression only a few cities—Louisville, Cincinnati, and Baltimore among others—had developed or were able to develop constructive programs for transients. Later in 1930 special programs were started in Rochester (New York), Cleveland, and other cities.

National Action

In November, 1930, the President's Emergency Committee for Employment (later replaced by the President's Organization on Unemployment Relief) was established to serve as a national clearing house and to advise on local efforts to promote employment and relieve unemployment. The official position in Washington at that time was that the primary responsibility for dealing with unemployment and caring for the unemployed lay with the local voluntary agencies, with governmental agencies lending what aid they could in the expectation that the depression would soon be over. Acting as assistant to the head of the President's Committee, Porter R. Lee, director of the New York School of Social Work, asked the Association to gather information on local developments and to prepare material on the administration of relief and on the care of

* Later, in 1932, the Association's Committee on the Homeless became part of the Committee on Care of Transients and Homeless appointed by the National Social Work Council.[13]

114

the homeless for the use of inexperienced workers in states and in local communities. Two pamphlets—*The Administration of Relief in Unemployment Emergencies*[14] and *The Care of the Homeless in Unemployment Emergencies*[15]—were ready for distribution in January, 1931, but two later requests from the Committee, one for a series of fact-finding studies of local situations as a basis for planning and interpretation and the other for expansion of Association field service to both organized and unorganized communities, had to wait until additional funds were available.

The program finally put into operation by the Association in the fall of 1931 was specifically defined as of an emergency, not of a permanent, nature, to be continued only as long as it was justified by needs and resources.

The plans were outlined at the Association's Annual Meeting in Minneapolis in June, 1931, and were described in the July *News Letter*:

> The special studies will consist largely of the collection, analysis, and summarizing of local studies and other material already existing, in order to place as little burden as possible upon member agencies. The reports will be edited and published by the Association, and made available to the field, to the President's Emergency Committee for Employment and to the Association's staff as a basis for meeting local inquiries. According to tentative plans these studies will include (a) case work material showing the effects of unemployment on family life and the ways in which families have met their emergencies; (b) a monthly summary and interpretation to the field of current changes in staff, agency, and community adjustments; (c) a special study of recent experience in community co-ordination of care of the homeless, which the President's Committee considers one of the most difficult problems of the past year; (d) special assistance to the Association's Pathfinding Committee on Governmental Relief Methods, in developing material both for the Committee's final report and for any preliminary reports which the Committee may desire to issue.
>
> The emergency expansion of Association field service will be undertaken with a clear recognition of the impossibility of meeting all demands from the many hundreds of local communities through direct visits from a national field staff. The Association will use a variety of methods, working as far as possible through existing state, regional, or local agencies, through the conference method, and through the employment for short periods of qualified persons from staffs of member agencies in different parts of the country for emergency services.[16]

In September, 1931, the Association added to its field staff and set up a Department of Special Studies under Arthur Dunham as direc-

115

tor and with Margaret Wead in charge of collecting, summarizing, and distributing material about local unemployment situations. This was a response not only to the request of the President's Committee but to the requests from the membership for information about ways in which family agencies were meeting problems common to all of them. A monthly schedule was sent to representative public and private agencies in large and small communities, totaling 172 agencies. The number answering varied from month to month, giving a vivid picture of changes in policies and practices growing out of the emergency.

The first *Monthly Summary* (so-called) was issued in December, 1931, and they continued for a two-year period. (Thirteen were issued between December, 1931, and December, 1933, the last two devoted to discussion of work relief programs.) These *Summaries* were sent to a mailing list of 10,000, including federal, state, and local officials as well as private agencies, and provided a substantial body of information about conditions throughout the country. Such a record of actual experience in planning and carrying out programs of large-scale relief had never before been available and it was of immediate use for comparing and evaluating different methods and planning next steps. The Department undertook a special study of the effects of unemployment on family life (based on case records from local agencies), made a study of community planning for homeless men and boys in sixteen cities,[17] gave staff service to the Pathfinding Committee on Governmental Relief Methods, and, with the advice of that Committee, prepared a pamphlet, *The Organization and Administration of Public Relief Agencies,* which had been requested by the President's Committee.[18]

The special emergency activities of the Association were tied in with its regular program. The regular field service was integrated with and supplemented by that of the emergency field staff. The additional field workers advised with state and regional groups and helped in the co-ordination of local efforts, using various approaches and the indirect method rather than attempting themselves to visit every local community in need of service. Both the regular and special staffs took part in inter-city and regional conferences, which were attended by workers from public and private agencies as well as by public officials.

116

The first *Monthly Summary* described some of the ways in which organizations had adjusted their plans to meet new demands, their flexibility in experimenting and in meeting changing situations. Many of these adjustments were thought of as "temporary" or "emergency."

> The most pressing question is the decision as to what agency will be responsible for the load of unemployment cases. The entire load has often been undertaken first by the family agency, responsibility being assumed by the public agency or newly created unemployment committee only as it became evident that the burden was too heavy for the family society. Often the next plan made was for the public agency or a newly created unemployment bureau to take over all unemployment cases at the time funds were released or the new machinery created. When such plans were actually put into operation, however, they frequently did not prove entirely satisfactory because of the fact that, even in families where unemployment was the outstanding problem, the case work care needed in addition to relief could not be given. On this account these mutually exclusive arrangements had to be modified.[19]

In community efforts the family society took its full share of responsibility not only for administering relief but for leadership in organizing resources and in co-ordinating the relief giving of miscellaneous groups. In a few cities—New York, Pittsburgh, and Chicago among others—the family society assigned unemployment cases to emergency staffs, operating from separate offices; in other cities, emergency staffs worked with the unemployed in the regular offices; and in still others the same staff served all applicants. Realignments of local resources took many forms: combinations, sometimes between private agencies and sometimes between public and private agencies, were formed in an effort to pool resources and stretch available staff and funds to the utmost, maintaining as far as possible a small division equipped to give needed casework service. A number of agencies had to increase or change office space to meet new conditions and even then there was often not sufficient room to provide minimum privacy for interviews. Extra money to meet relief needs was raised by the community chest or by the family society or, in a number of instances, by securing grants from governmental funds.

Wendell F. Johnson, director of the Social Service Federation in Toledo, Ohio, described the problem:

117

Even more difficult than the financing of relief has been the task of actually dealing with the day to day applications for assistance from thousands of families who were seeking outside aid for the first time; the task of giving an unhurried individualized interview to those thousands of applicants, supplying leadership and direction in some plan by which they might keep their home intact and their family life as normal as possible. . . . In other words, the case work job adjusted to an enormously increased case load was the greatest problem of all.[20]

Family social work both nationally and locally was aware that the anomaly of widespread distress in a land of plenty could not be met by relief alone or by casework but only through careful planning on a national scale. The Association Board made this conviction clear at its meeting in October, 1931:

We recognize that the vast majority of those whom we are now serving are afflicted by social and economic conditions beyond their personal control. While we can do much to assist such families in the development of their own capacity to meet economic distress, we are equally interested in a sound community program directed toward the causes of poverty. We are not content with palliative measures of relief, necessary as they may be, unless they are accompanied by a concerted and thoughtful attempt gradually to rectify basic conditions.

This resolution was incorporated in a statement sent to boards and staffs of the 238 member societies with the request that they comment for or against the last paragraph:

While we pledge our best efforts toward the relief of distress during the difficult period before us, we call upon the civic and industrial leaders of America for concerted effort and wide participation in planning measures which, under proper safeguards in the public interest, may ultimately bring greater security in employment and a more adequate distribution of purchasing power among the masses of American people.

The great majority (2,773) of the 2,891 laymen and social workers who expressed their views on the statement gave it their approval.

The statement was not intended to bind the agencies to any particular social or economic program but rather to stimulate discussion, and in this it was successful. The *News Letter* of March, 1932, reported that there was considerable comment in the press and the local societies followed up with interpretation of pertinent data to arouse "public interest in the fundamental problems which lie beyond relief giving."

118

By the summer of 1931 it had become obvious that existing agencies and resources were not able to cope with the mounting load of relief and that reinforcements must be found. At that time Linton B. Swift, executive director of the Association, joined with executives of other national agencies in an Informal Social Work Conference on Federal Action on Unemployment. A subcommittee known as the Steering Committee, of which Mr. Swift was also a member, was appointed to gather material on local conditions throughout the country to be used to persuade Congress of the need for federal help. Senators Edward P. Costigan and Robert M. LaFollette, Jr., were already interested in the idea of federal action but the bills they presented to Congress were defeated. A different type of federal help was provided in the summer of 1932 when the Reconstruction Finance Corporation was authorized to lend money to the states for direct relief and work relief. The amount of money appropriated—$300,000,000—was less than was needed and the RFC assumed no responsibility for standards of administration, although a field staff of competent social workers was prepared to assist the governors in setting up plans for operation within the states.

Several of the states had already set up Temporary Emergency Relief Administrations—the first of them in New York in September, 1931—which were making funds for relief available to local units. Although these programs were still "temporary" or "emergency," the funds from the states, and from the Reconstruction Finance Corporation, made possible the rapid development of relief agencies under public auspices and initiated new patterns in public relief administration.

The Association employed additional field staff to meet the many requests for consultation from local and state agencies and to develop regional meetings for discussion of the practical problems of organization, administration, personnel, and maintenance of standards as well as co-operative arrangements with state agencies in the field service to local communities. The field program was co-ordinated as closely as possible with the activities of the American Public Welfare Association (organized in 1930) and other national agencies, with the understanding that the Association would be concerned primarily with local situations and their relationship to state public welfare and relief systems.

119

As the unemployment situation continued unabated—in some ways growing worse because people suffered from exhaustion of savings and equally from exhaustion of morale—the problem of qualified personnel for relief administration, always acute, became increasingly difficult, especially for the newly organized public agencies needing competent staff. All the agencies had been forced to employ workers who had neither training nor experience and had enlisted the help of volunteers as casework aides, as clinic escorts, as receptionists, and as clerical workers. Orientation, at least minimum training, and good supervision were essential for all these workers if the unemployed were to get the kind of help they so sorely needed.

All the members of the Association staff shared in helping local agencies make and carry out plans to maintain continuing programs for staff development, adapted to the local need. These plans varied from simple orientation sessions to seminars and institutes for experienced workers. Outlines for training courses, case records for teaching, printed material ranging from the most elementary to the most advanced, were prepared and made available through the Association staff, along with pamphlets and special articles in *The Family* and the *News Letter*. Members of the Association staff supplied leaders for study groups and round tables, frequently leading such groups themselves. Studies of salaries, of personnel practices, of recruiting and training conducted by the Association on a year-in year-out basis were continued in spite of the pressures of the emergency, and focused specifically on the current problems. These studies provided material that was of immediate use in strengthening staff and maintaining standards.

In spite of consistently high case loads and lack of time, caseworkers themselves played an active part in what might be called self-training—in studying and evaluating what they were doing and trying to develop more effective ways of helping. Linton B. Swift pointed out that this self-evaluation and analysis contributed to "the development of new skills in handling large numbers of individuals with a light touch, with a careful selection and adaptation of those case work processes which seem appropriate in short time contacts and infuse a case work approach into mass relief." [21]

120

The very necessity of meeting limitations of time and resources proved to be assets. Margaret Wead, editor of the *Monthly Summary*, commented in *The Family*:

> Through the exigencies of our present situation client and worker have been drawn into a kind of working partnership which, although always part of our case work goal, was never so nearly realized before, Agencies have come to see more than ever that they can do little that is truly effective unless the client seeks help and goes with the worker every step of the way.[22]

Mr. Swift and his associates on the Steering Committee, which had now been merged with the Committee on Governmental Relief of the American Association of Social Workers, did not give up hope of some federal action that would bring continuing rather than temporary federal assistance. Social workers the country over, who had firsthand knowledge of what was happening to individuals and families, of the loss of morale and self-respect that accompanied the loss of a job, of the sheer physical suffering from inadequate food, poor housing, and lack of clothing, told their stories to the Committee members or went to Washington themselves to give their testimony. Finally, in May, 1933, the Federal Emergency Relief Act was passed by Congress and signed by President Franklin Delano Roosevelt. This Act established a Federal Emergency Relief Administration with an administrator authorized "to make grants to the several states to aid in meeting the costs of furnishing relief and work relief and in relieving the hardship and suffering caused by unemployment."

Arthur Dunham explained the significance of the new legislation:

> The Federal Emergency Relief Act of 1933 . . . reversed an historic federal policy . . . based on the belief that the federal government had no constitutional power to grant funds for . . . welfare purposes. . . . It accepted federal responsibility, supplied federal leadership, and appropriated federal funds for unemployment relief in the emergency.[23]

In June, 1933, Harry L. Hopkins, FERA administrator, issued a ruling that, beginning August 1, 1933, federal emergency relief funds were to be administered only by public agencies. This ruling was in line with the traditional philosophy of charity organization and family social work—that government funds should be administered by government agencies officially responsible to the public. But the stress and strain of the last few years, lack of funds,

121

and lack of staff had seemed, in a number of local communities, to justify some form of subsidy from public funds to private agencies in order to get relief to those in need as humanely and quickly as possible. The arrangements were usually thought of as temporary, and had been modified as conditions changed, particularly with the organization of state emergency relief in a number of states and the consequent growth of local public relief agencies.

The *Monthly Summary* described agency setup in a number of fairly typical communities a few months before the Federal Emergency Relief Act was passed:

> In 21 cities [out of 76 reporting] one organization is largely responsible for the whole relief program. Seven of these have family welfare agencies but no public department. (Cleveland, Houston, and Baltimore are in this group.) At least part of the relief funds in all these seven cities comes from public sources. In three of the 21 cities there are no private welfare societies. . . . In four other cities the family welfare society is really administering the relief but there is a public department with limited responsibilities. . . . Six cities report joint staff arrangements.[24]

Forty-seven of 67 private societies sending information about the source of their income were at this time using public funds in some way. In a number of these places this was a recent development. In 28 there was some arrangement whereby both public and private agencies shared the responsibility for individual families. In Milwaukee, for instance, the family society requisitioned relief from the public department for individual families much as did the department's own staff. There was also evidence of an increase in public relief agencies. One agency reported:

> The County Welfare Department was organized December 1, 1932. There is a spirit of patience and good will which promises much for the future. . . . At the present moment the Department of Public Aid is being reorganized on a case work basis and contemplates the employment of at least eight trained and experienced caseworkers, one to act as a supervisor, the others to be district secretaries . . . and [it is hoped] to decrease the case load so that no worker will have over 150 families. . . . Even in this first year of tremendous growth it [the public department] has moved slowly but steadily in the right direction.[25]

The ruling of the FERA administrator limiting federal funds to governmental agencies meant that those private agencies that had formed some joint financial arrangement with public agencies must lose their share of public funds—unless it came from sources not receiving federal money—or themselves become public agencies. With the deadline of August 1 only six weeks away no time was lost in trying to work out agency realignments to meet the requirements of the ruling. The experiences of 59 cities described in the *Monthly Summary* in October, 1933, give an idea of the variety of adjustments that were made:

> In 17 of these 59 cities new public relief agencies have been established. . . . In 13 they have taken over work previously done by private agencies . . . and in four the work of public departments. In six of 59 cities a public agency is the only organization in the family welfare and relief field. Six months ago, three of these cities had no public agency.[26]

Unemployment relief was now almost wholly a public responsibility. Private agencies were generally concerned with casework service to families especially needing it. It was found that in 23 cities of the above group there was some sharing of responsibility. In 14 of them the private agency indicated that it gave special casework service to what were otherwise public agency relief cases. Nine agencies reported lending their executives to public agencies. Supervisors, district secretaries, and other staff members also were lent. In addition to loans, ten agencies transferred individual staff members, seven agencies their emergency staffs, and three the entire staff. Twenty-three agencies out of 43, compared with 47 out of 76 six months earlier, had arrangements for public relief and private services. Private agencies were eager to help develop the new public agencies on as sound a basis as possible.[27]

While things had settled into a more definite pattern than was true at the beginning of FERA, they were still far from static. A major task of clarification, of definition of function, of building up staff and standards of work lay ahead, a task for which the Association and local public and private family agencies had a responsibility.

References

1. *A Perspective of Family Social Work,* American Association for Organizing Family Social Work, Quarterly Bulletin, December, 1926, p. 11.
2. *American Association for Organizing Family Social Work News Letter,* Vol. II, No. 1 (1927), p. 4.

3. *The Time to Plan Is Now,* Report of the Committee on Industrial Problems, American Association for Organizing Family Social Work, New York, 1929.

4. Mary E. Richmond, "Emergency Relief in Times of Unemployment," *The Long View,* eds. Joanna C. Colcord and Ruth Z. S. Mann, Russell Sage Foundation, New York, 1930, p. 510.

5. Linton B. Swift, "The Relief Problem in Family Social Work," *The Family,* Vol. X, No. 1 (1929), p. 10.

6. Philip Klein, *The Burden of Unemployment,* Russell Sage Foundation, New York, 1923.

7. Joanna C. Colcord, *Cash Relief,* Russell Sage Foundation, New York, 1936.

8. Leah H. Feder, *Unemployment Relief in Periods of Depression,* Russell Sage Foundation, New York, 1936.

9. Caroline Bedford, "Effect of an Unemployment Situation on Family Societies," *Proceedings, National Conference of Social Work: 1931,* University of Chicago Press, Chicago, 1931, p. 202.

10. *Family Welfare Association of America News Letter,* Vol. V, No. 6 (1930), p. 23.

11. *Ibid.*

12. *FWAA News Letter,* Vol. VII, No. 5 (1932), p. 23.

13. Joanna C. Colcord, "Unemployment Relief, 1929–1932," *The Family,* Vol. XIII, No. 8 (1932), p. 273; see also Editorial Notes of same issue, p. 284.

14. Margaret E. Rich, *The Administration of Relief in Unemployment Emergencies,* Family Welfare Association of America, New York, 1931.

15. Harriet E. Anderson and Margaret E. Rich, *The Care of the Homeless in Unemployment Emergencies,* Family Welfare Association of America, New York, 1931.

16. *FWAA News Letter,* Vol. VI, No. 5 (1931), p. 22.

17. Robert S. Wilson, *Community Planning for Homeless Men and Boys,* Family Welfare Association of America, New York, 1932.

18. Rose Porter, *The Organization and Administration of Public Relief Agencies,* Family Welfare Association of America, New York, 1931.

19. "Unemployment Relief Experience," *FWAA Monthly Summary,* December, 1931, p. 2.

20. Wendell F. Johnson, "How Case Working Agencies Have Met Unemployment," *Proceedings, NCSW: 1931,* p. 191.

21. Linton B. Swift, "Social Work and the Family," *The Family,* Vol. XIII, No. 6 (1932), p. 213.

22. Margaret Wead, "Drifts in Unemployment Relief," *The Family,* Vol. XIII, No. 7 (1932), p. 223.

23. Arthur Dunham, "Public Assistance in the United States," *The Public Assistance Worker,* ed. Russell Kurtz, Russell Sage Foundation, New York, 1938, p. 20.

24. *FWAA Monthly Summary,* April, 1933, p. 9.

25. *Ibid.,* p. 16.

26. *FWAA Monthly Summary,* October, 1933, p. 70.

27. *Ibid.,* p. 71.

VIII. Period of Transition

WITH THE ASSUMPTION by the government of the major responsibility for unemployment relief, both public and private agencies were faced with the need for action on a number of important issues. Among the problems requiring attention were the stabilization and regularization of state and local public administrative units, the definition and clarification of the roles of private and public agencies, and the unscrambling of some agencies that were trying to be both public and private. Other urgent matters were the strengthening of casework content in programs, the knitting together of lay and professional leadership in both public and private agencies, and the recruiting and training of much-needed personnel.

The situation was further complicated for agencies, and for the unemployed persons in need of help, by the emergency nature of many of the governmental provisions for unemployment relief. Changes in the federal program were made frequently and a series of work projects for young people and for the "employable" unemployed was established by the federal government as it gradually withdrew from participation in direct relief.* Joint thinking by public

---

* The projects included: Civil Works Administration (CWA), 1933–34; Works Progress Administration (WPA), 1935–43; Civilian Conservation Corps (CCC), 1933–43; National Youth Administration (NYA), 1935–43.[1]

125

and voluntary agencies, which had characterized so much of the planning of the previous four years, was now needed more than ever. Each agency, public and private alike, had a stake in the development of the other. In the December, 1933, issue of *The Family*, Karl de Schweinitz said, "Public and private agencies are mutually dependent upon one another, and, if we did not know this before, certainly the past four years of unemployment relief have demonstrated it beyond peradventure of a doubt." [2]

In 1933 the Family Welfare Association of America held a number of regional round tables—that unparalleled device for what an Association report called "a constant interchange of thought and of co-operation in meeting current issues and in deepening and carrying forward the whole field of family social work." [3] The titles of these conferences, in which both public and private agency workers took part, indicated the willingness on the part of both to face new developments and to abandon outworn traditions: The New Future in Family Welfare Work (Middle Atlantic and Southern Regions), Family Welfare in a Changing World (Rocky Mountain), Present Trends Among Public and Private Family Agencies (a series held in different parts of the country). To meet the increasing desire—on the part of both laymen and staff workers in large and small communities—for participation in such round tables and in other affairs of the national organization, the Association adopted a plan broadening the base of eligibility for individual membership, making it no longer elective, as it had been when it was inaugurated in 1919. The new plan adopted in 1933, which established qualifications for both "Professional Members" and "Associate Members," was of special value to family social workers who had jobs in public welfare or in other agencies not members of the Association. [4]

New Alignments

From these group discussions and from other sources Linton B. Swift, the general director of the Association, assembled material that he presented in a pamphlet, *New Alignments Between Public and Private Agencies in a Community Family Welfare and Relief Program*, as a basis for "clarification of the working relationships

126

of public and private agencies." [5] Mr. Swift made it clear that "no single and universally applicable pattern is or can be offered for a uniform division of specific services between public and private agencies" and that the ideas presented were to be thought of "not as a final product but as a point of departure for local study and discussion." He asserted:

> It is a mistake to assume that the present relief pressure is only temporary and that business and industrial recovery will soon enable us to return to the more or less even tenor of our old ways of doing things. The old days are gone; we face a new future alignment. With any conceivable improvement in economic conditions, we shall have four or five million unemployed for at least the next five years, with an aftermath of human wreckage such as we have never known in any previous depression. Both public and private agencies will have all they can do in facing new problems and in finding new ways to meet them.[6]

Mr. Swift also pointed out that a "rounded family welfare and relief program . . . requires both public and private agencies, each supplementing the other, with co-operation and an interflow of services between them." He suggested that any agreement as to division of responsibility must be reviewed and modified to meet the requirements of changing community conditions and for this purpose frequent, preferably regular, discussions by a joint committee were essential; that, in general, the public agency was the official instrument of society in mitigating social and economic inequalities which society had not yet corrected, while the private agency was concerned in meeting needs not yet recognized by the whole community and its particular contribution was a qualitative and experimental job. "Public and private agencies thus have a reciprocal responsibility, each to assist the other, in the readjustments which lie ahead." [7]

The pamphlet was immediately useful to schools of social work, to agency staffs and boards, and to councils of social agencies, and the first edition was sold out within two months.

Questions relating to new alignments or adjustments in community programs for family welfare were to be of vital concern in the following years. At an informal meeting of representatives of large-city agencies convened by the Association in April, 1934, it was evident that all those present—state and local public officials and private agency workers—were feeling the pressure of the unsettled situation. With the discontinuance of the Civil Works Administration in March there had been an appreciable increase in applications for relief, which was further augmented by those of persons who, with the prolongation of the depression, had come to the end of their resources. At the same time, the general picture of state and local resources was depressing so far as funds and available staff were concerned.

The discussions at the conference of large-city agencies covered a wide range of subjects of immediate concern to both public and private agencies: adequacy of relief; need for qualified personnel, particularly in key positions in the public agencies; well-defined working relationships between public and private agencies; and, as basic to present and future planning, interpretation to local communities of these problems and the steps necessary to meet them. At the final session the group expressed its feeling that many of the measures that had been discussed were still very much in a transition stage and that it would be unwise to crystallize opinions or recommendations at this time. Although the conference participants expressed the need for further and continued exploration both by themselves and by other smaller local groups, they agreed on the following points:

> Any family welfare agency ideally should give both full relief and family case work service to all families accepted by it for care. Anything short of this should be regarded either as an experiment or as a matter of expediency. As rapidly as possible the division of field between the public and private agencies should be worked out on the basis of the development of actual capacity to give differentiated service and the co-operative steps taken towards that end should be definitely planned and stated. [In planning for the future it might be possible for a public welfare department to develop under its own auspices a separate bureau to which might be referred relief cases requiring special services.] . . . combined efforts will not even approximately meet community needs for some time to come. Therefore each agency has a reciprocal responsibility for interpreting and supporting the work of the other in relation to the family social work needs of the community . . . the casework practice of all agencies engaged in family casework, public and private, makes it desirable that qualified and trained case workers should be used for intake service and for agency interpretation at the point of intake . . . a permanent national, state, and local public welfare program is essential and . . . every effort should be made to achieve [such permanent organization] . . . to integrate in that program the desirable features of the present emergency program, and to develop the strongest possible support in states and communities for these objectives.[8]

Further clarification of what was practical as well as desirable in readjustments came from local discussions between public and private agencies and from state and regional meetings sponsored by the Association. One such meeting, held in Cleveland in March, 1934, primarily for board members of family agencies in Ohio, was concerned with the importance of lay understanding and support of community programs for family welfare, of the need for adequate relief—food, clothing, shelter—and for personal service. Similar meetings were held in other parts of the country either on a regional or state-wide basis. Later in the year an all-day meeting on Family Life and National Recovery was held in New York City with an attendance of 460 persons, half of them volunteers or board members, from ninety-seven cities.[9]

Among the formal papers presented at that meeting was the summary of a study of the effect of economic unemployment on family life, made by a board and staff committee of the Philadelphia Family Society. In general, the seventy-five families studied— young, middle-aged, and old, and of many nationalities and religions—showed a tendency to withdraw from the world and fall back upon the shelter of their homes. The families studied were all under the care of the Family Society and most of them owed their homes to the relief obtained from that source. The report stated:

> If the study had been made of a group of families unable to secure cash or some other form of relief that would enable them to maintain their homes, many instances would have been found in which the family had been separated . . . or in which the entire family had been taken in by relatives. There would be less hope for them; for some, it would perhaps mean the end of all family relationship. . . . The encouraging aspect is that so large a number have found a balance for their insecurity in what the home means to them. Whatever else has been lost, family unity continues.[10]

Material gathered by the Association for the meeting on Family Life and National Recovery from more than a hundred local family agencies presented a mixed picture:

> Studies of groups of families in several cities indicate in many instances a tendency to withdraw from their customary contacts with church, friends, and recreational opportunities not only because of lack of money and consequent lack of clothes but because "they have no heart for such things." . . . To some families this has come to mean a greater dependence on one another, a finding of new resources in the

129

home. To others this withdrawing has increased family irritation, quarreling, nagging to the point where one or another—usually the father or an adolescent child—leaves home either temporarily or permanently.[11]

Other agencies reported that families felt a loss of prestige, tension, and a sense of emotional insecurity increased by the general trend in industry to refuse to employ women over thirty and men over forty. These personal reactions were thought to be areas of human need which public relief could not meet. Porter R. Lee called them "areas that lie outside its necessary preoccupation with mass relief, outside its statutory limitations, outside its adaptability to many human problems which are covered by reticence and sensibilities." [12] These were considered areas in which private family societies, freed from the burden of overwhelming relief pressures, could offer their services: social casework to assist individuals in removing their own handicaps and community activities leading to removal of external barriers to individual growth.

The 1935 Annual Meeting of the Association, which was held in Cincinnati, offered a much needed opportunity to review and evaluate current developments and to consider next steps. This was the first time the Association had held its annual meeting apart from the National Conference and attendance was limited—also for the first time—to individual members and to delegates from member agencies. For the next few years the Association held its annual meetings in the same city as the National Conference but in advance of those sessions; after 1938 the Association, while continuing to participate in the Conference, held a Biennial Meeting of its own membership at a different time of year.

The meeting in Cincinnati, like the fiftieth anniversary celebration eight years before in Buffalo, emphasized the paramount interest and function of family social work in relation to the understanding of the family and the development and application of skills in strengthening family life. The relationships between public and private agencies came in for more attention than at the 1927 meeting. The need for joint planning committees and the responsibility of both public and private agencies to contribute to programs for social change in so far as they affect family life were stressed. Case records were studied and a number of practical sub-

130

jects such as methods of interpretation and ways of developing lay and staff leadership were discussed. The pooling of experience on these concrete matters was particularly important in view of the general governmental relief situation, which was going through some critical changes.

On August 14, 1935, the Social Security Act was signed by the President of the United States. It provided for participation by the federal government in insurance programs for the unemployed and the aged and in public assistance programs for the aged, dependent children, and the blind, under the executive charge of a Social Security Board. Other provisions of the Act were related to maternal and child welfare, vocational rehabilitation, and health, to be administered by the Children's Bureau, the Office of Education, and the Public Health Service. The Social Security Act was described by Eveline M. Burns as "the most ambitious and comprehensive attempt ever made by the American government to promote the economic security of the individual." [13]

The Federal Emergency Relief Administration had established the principle of federal participation in public assistance in an emergency. The Social Security Act implied "the assumption by the federal government of responsibility for the economic in addition to the political security of Americans as a permanent and not merely an emergency undertaking." [14] The wide range of security measures in the national plan formed an imposing bulwark against insecurity, but it was recognized that even when it was fully implemented many individuals and families would still be exposed to economic need.

Responsibility for Relief

Arthur Dunham has commented on the period preceding the passage of the Social Security Act:

> The months following the withdrawal of the federal government [from participation in direct relief] were marked by great confusion in the field of direct relief. Some states—among them New York, Pennsylvania, and Michigan—continued their state relief administrations and their appropriations of state funds for relief. Unemployment relief showed an increasing tendency to merge with general public assistance and to embrace much or most of the traditional poor relief load. In

131

other states—such as New Jersey and Illinois—the state relief administrations came to an end and the responsibility for general public assistance reverted to the local poor relief authorities. . . . Where state aid was
withdrawn, local governments frequently found themselves unable to
handle the relief load with any pretense of adequacy.[15]

In a number of communities where the situation had become
critical, there was a tendency on the part of the public to expect
the private agency to take over responsibility for relief and the
societies were turning to the Association for help in deciding what
should be done. In May, 1935, the whole problem was placed
before the Association Board, which spent the better part of two
days discussing the many implications of the situation and preparing a statement for the use of the membership. The Board was
convinced that resources that could be expected from voluntary
funds were so limited that there was little possibility of private
agencies' meeting the relief needs that had been thrown upon states
and communities by the change in federal policy. In addition to
the unmet needs of local residents, many communities were again
faced with an influx of transients since the federal transient program had been discontinued, and transients were sleeping in parks
or jails and resorting to panhandling.

A statement outlining the Board's conclusions was prepared for
the membership. In part, it said:

> . . . all available statistics indicate that only from one to three per cent
> of the total relief needs now are being met from private funds and . . .
> that even before the depression over 70 per cent of relief expenditures
> came from tax funds. Any attempt upon the part of private agencies
> to assume an overwhelming relief burden will almost inevitably wreck
> the programs of constructive and preventive service which many such
> agencies have been better able to develop since they were free from
> previous community relief burdens. Any public impression that pri-
> vate effort could carry increased relief burdens would serve not only
> to retard promising developments in local public agencies, but would
> also serve as an easy excuse for inertia on the part of higher state and
> local public authorities. . . .
> It was recognized that, whatever its own broader conception of its
> services may be, the private family welfare agency is still generally tied
> up in the public mind primarily with economic need; that is, with
> relief administration. Although as an ultimate goal social case work
> service is potentially useful to all persons who have difficulty in adjust-
> ing themselves to their fellows, regardless of their economic situation,
> it was recognized that the private agency . . . must generally start from
> where it now stands, continuing to assist many families in which finan-
> cial distress is related to other family problems. But, as an immediate
> and practical goal, it can gradually extend its services to the . . .

132

marginal-income group who may not need relief but who cannot afford to pay for services which are vitally needed. . . .

Although a few private agencies are now attempting to develop a family case work program without using relief funds of their own, members of the Board felt that private agencies in general will need relief resources not only for so-called economically dependent families, but also for families in the marginal-income group with special or temporary needs requiring financial assistance. . . .

Recognizing the critical situation which will exist in many states and communities if, with the cessation of federal support, emergency relief machinery is merely scrapped with nothing to take its place, there was among the members of the Board a consensus . . . that wherever local circumstances made it possible, citizens interested in public and private agencies alike should join in a rallying of community forces for the development or the strengthening of permanent state and local public welfare administration.

The summary of the Board's discussion was sent to the boards of all member societies with a request for comments and suggestions. In general, the societies agreed that private agencies neither could nor should attempt to take over any part of the community relief responsibility then being carried by public agencies and that all agencies should give the strongest possible support to the development of high standards of personnel in local departments of public welfare. A number of the local boards proceeded at once to mobilize community forces in support of the governmental relief program. Releasing or lending of private agency staff to strengthen the public agency, which has already been mentioned, continued. Porter R. Lee commented, in 1934: "Two years ago the majority of our most competent workers were in the employ of private social agencies. Within that period these workers have been steadily drafted by developing public departments. This transfer of personnel, in my judgment, is one of the greatest services which private agencies have rendered the cause of social welfare in this country." [16]

Recruiting and Training

Desirable as these transfers were, they obviously did not meet the demand for additional workers urgently needed in the expanding social service and relief programs under private and public auspices. Earlier, the Federal Emergency Relief Administration and several state relief departments had set up a variety of training plans for public agency staffs, either programs for definite training on the job or grants for limited periods of study at schools of social work. Many of the private societies which had been forced to reduce or to give up training activities in the early years of the depression now resumed them. In 1935, fifty-nine agencies accepted 867 students for field work from thirty-six schools of social work. Of these, 151 students received agency fellowships. The next year ninety-two agencies accepted 1,010 students.

In addition, family societies began to give more attention to educational opportunities for staff members through providing for attendance at conferences, institutes, and school courses; in 1935 the Association sponsored forty-seven institutes, regional and inter-city conferences, and other group meetings, the majority of them attended by persons from public as well as private agencies, by board members as well as professional staff.

As a further help in development of staff, the Association employed Mabel Uzzell as part-time personnel director. Miss Uzzell, who also gave part time to the Joint Vocational Service, a placement bureau for social workers, began her work with the Association January 1, 1936. She gave consultation to agencies and prospective candidates and stimulated national and local plans for recruiting and training workers.

The Association conferred with both federal and state officials on questions of personnel and training and other matters and, without committing the member societies, continued to express its conviction that the federal government should develop a comprehensive, co-ordinated program of relief and security for all categories of dependents, to be participated in by states and local communities. Locally most of the societies took an active part in developing the federal and state personnel programs and in mobilizing lay and professional support for the stabilization of public welfare—support that had to be continually renewed as staff retrenchment or lowering of relief standards was threatened.

Joint Committees

Joint committees, often under a council of social agencies, proved their value not only for setting forth fundamental principles on

134

division of responsibilities between public and private family agencies but for discussion of individual case situations. Procedures were discussed in a 1937 issue of the *News Letter:*

> . . . The most successful procedure from the point of view of actual working arrangements and service to families seems to be a real thinking through by a joint committee of public and private groups as to what is needed and practicable in the specific local situation. Such co-operative case committees have functioned in many of the communities that have developed an effective relationship. The procedures of these committees have naturally differed—some have gone at the problem from the point of view of determining categories that may be cared for entirely by either public or private agency and those on which joint activity would seem to be advisable. Others have proceeded from the slower approach of the case-by-case discussion, bringing up individual situations and considering whether or not supplementary service by the private agency would be helpful.[17]

Such case discussions resulted in better understanding, by each, of the other agency's strengths and limitations and made for better interpretation to clients of the services each had to offer. By mutual agreement the private society might, on the basis of the discussion, give service to a family that was receiving relief from public funds, but such an arrangement was usually seen as temporary, pending the day when the public agency itself could provide such needed service. Indirectly, such case discussions resulted in division of responsibility or the joint carrying of responsibility on the basis of what was likely to be best for families and individuals.

National and Local Activities

Following the establishment of the Federal Emergency Relief Administration in 1933 and the American Public Welfare Association in 1930, each undertaking certain consultative functions for governmental agencies, the Association discontinued in 1934 the special field service to public agencies it had started in 1931. The Department of Special Studies, however, which had met a need long felt by the membership, was continued with Margaret Wead as director. The Department of Studies and Information, as it was now called, greatly facilitated the gathering and distribution of information on trends and special projects in agency programs. Working with the department, the Association's Committee on Statistics and Information Service developed a form for the use of member societies in making annual reports of activities to the Association which provided an extremely valuable, well-organized body of factual information about what was going on in the field, equally useful to the agencies and the Association.

These yearly reports gave an over-all picture of the gradual reshaping of the programs of private family agencies, of staff turnover, board and committee activities, lists of local studies, division of work with public agencies, and so on. For many societies the transition from giving relief with casework service as incidental, to giving casework service with relief as incidental, was not made without difficulties. Some of what was undertaken was experimental, some of it was opportunistic and tended to be short-lived, but there was also gradual development of activities to meet demonstrated needs, some of long standing, some only recently recognized. Many of these activities became part of permanent programs.

Several agencies had previously provided homemakers, also known as visiting housekeepers or substitute mothers, for motherless families or for families where the mother was ill. At this period the Department of Studies and Information reported that inquiries received about establishing such a service were increasing.

Special bureaus for the aged were set up in a few societies, and in 1936 the Association organized an informal conference on the problems of old age with Ruth Hill, Deputy Commissioner in Charge of the Old-Age Security Division in the New York City Department of Welfare, as chairman and Mr. McLean as staff consultant. Service to old people was by no means an innovation in family agencies but it had been little explored and the committee hoped to assemble material from case records which would be of value to both caseworkers and boards.[18]

Some agencies experimented with group activities, such as meetings for mothers who came together for several sessions to discuss the care of children and other family problems. There were other special services in different societies; for example, help with employment, with re-education, and with small business ventures, usually with the advice of committees of employment managers or other expert groups. The yearly reports showed that agencies were gradually integrating these and other special projects with their

136

regular work or adding them primarily for what they could contribute to casework.

The possibilities of a wider use of family casework, of reaching people who needed not economic help but help with their social adjustments, led a few societies to set up a "family consultation service." This was part of a trend to get away from the implication of charity and relief. This trend showed itself in the changes made in titles of agencies, so that by 1936 the majority of the Association's members were using "family service" or "family welfare." These titles were considered more descriptive of their work than "charity" and the changes carried out, at long last, the recommendation made in 1919 by the Association Committee on Future Scope and Policy. The new titles suggested the scope of the societies' work and interest in a way that the old titles had failed to do. Stanley P. Davies, president of the Association, pointed out:

> We did not become family societies and family social workers out of a process of reasoning about the importance of the family, nor did we put emphasis upon the family just because as an aggregation of human beings in one household it presents a convenient unit for working purposes. It was rather that, as people revealed to us the problems really on their minds and hearts, these problems almost invariably led right back to the family and to family relationships. The individual we were trying to help took us there.[19]

The re-emphasis on scope and function was accompanied by a revival of interest in the study of the family and of what family casework had to offer for the enhancement of family life. Such study had been stressed at the Buffalo conference on family life in 1927, but was more or less ignored under the pressures of the unemployment relief situation. The program of the 1938 Annual Meeting represented an attempt to clarify and define the peculiar contribution of family casework and to explore methods of productive research in the development of precision both in body of knowledge and in professional skills. Already a number of societies had undertaken studies that helped to clarify the function of the agencies and the new orientation in practice. These were evolving, as Florence T. Waite pointed out, from "a greater understanding of the fundamental structure underlying the emotional life, coupled with more sensitive appreciation of individual needs."

137

She continued, "Delicate technical skills are being evolved to meet more precisely and effectively problems arising from the emotional life of the client. This increased understanding is illuminating the case worker's whole range of practice...." [20]

Some of these developments were reflected in a review of agency activities by the Membership Committee over a two-year period and in the revised requirements for membership adopted in 1938. In drafting the requirements, the Committee members had in mind a description of the kind of agency setting in which the client can best be served. They affirmed:

1. That the basic activity [of a family agency] is family case work of a sort that is progressively adapted to growth in knowledge and to the needs of clients.
2. That the means for effecting this activity is a responsible governing body and a developing staff which has the skill to give competent service.
3. That the board and the staff show concern for the improvement of social conditions affecting family life in their own community.
The phrases—growth in knowledge, developing staff, improvement of social conditions—clearly indicate the dynamic quality of these standards. [21]

In the first Annual Report of the Association Mr. McLean had written, "We recognize no standard excepting that of constant improvement." In 1938 the Membership Committee voiced a similar conviction, at least by implication, and added criteria for measuring the vitality of an agency and its willingness to participate with the Association in coping with the problems of the field as a whole, setting up standards basically so sound that the intervening years have called for only a few minor changes.

References

1. Arthur E. Fink, "The Development of Social Work—Public Welfare," *The Field of Social Work*, Henry Holt, New York, 1949 (rev.), chap. I. See also: Josephine C. Brown, *Public Relief 1929–1939*, Henry Holt, New York, 1940; Fred K. Hoehler, "Public Welfare," *Social Work Year Book, 1937*, ed. Russell H. Kurtz, Russell Sage Foundation, New York, 1937, pp. 387–392.
2. Karl de Schweinitz, "Tomorrow in Family Social Work," *The Family*, Vol. XIV, No. 8 (1933), p. 264.
3. *Family Social Work in Transition*, Report of Activities—1935, 1936, and 1937, Family Welfare Association of America, New York, 1938, p. 17.
4. *Family Welfare Association of America News Letter*, Vol. VIII, No. 3 (1933), p. 18.

5. Linton B. Swift, *New Alignments Between Public and Private Agencies in a Community Family Welfare and Relief Program*, Family Welfare Association of America, New York, 1934, p. 1.

6. *Ibid.*, p. 10.

7. *Ibid.*, pp. 19, 11–12, 8.

8. *Report on Big Cities Conference, April 18–21, 1934*, Family Welfare Association of America, New York, 1934, pp. 12–13.

9. *Family Life and National Recovery:* "The Layman Looks at Family Social Work," by Mrs. John D. Rockefeller, 3d; "Do Professional Standards Help Families?," by Dorothy C. Kahn; "Family Life and Recovery," by Dr. Harry Emerson Fosdick; "Relation of Public and Private Agencies," by Mary L. Gibbons; "Family Consultation Service as a Function of a Family Agency," by Dr. Julien E. Benjamin; "The Effect of Economic Unemployment on Family Life," Report of a Committee of the Family Society of Philadelphia. Family Welfare Association of America, New York, 1935.

10. "The Effect of Economic Unemployment on Family Life," Report of a Committee of the Family Society of Philadephia, *Family Life and National Recovery (supra)*, pp. 3–4, 29.

11. *Family Social Work in a Changing World*, Family Welfare Association of America, New York, 1934, p. 2.

12. Porter R. Lee, "Social Case Work," *The Family*, Vol. XV, No. 7 (1934), p. 202.

13. Eveline M. Burns, "Social Security Act," *Social Work Year Book, 1937*, ed. Russell H. Kurtz, Russell Sage Foundation, New York, 1937, p. 472.

14. *Ibid.*, pp. 477–478.

15. Arthur Dunham, "Public Assistance in the United States," *The Public Assistance Worker*, ed. Russell H. Kurtz, Russell Sage Foundation, New York, 1938, pp. 23–24.

16. Porter R. Lee, *op. cit.*, p. 203.

17. *FWAA News Letter*, Vol. XII, No. 2 (1937), p. 5.

18. *FWAA News Letter*, Vol. XI, No. 6 (1936), p. 36. See also: Ruth Hill, "Social Case Work as Applied to Old Age Assistance," *The Family*, Vol. XVI, No. 6 (1935), pp. 170–172; "The Adventure of Old Age," editorial notes, *The Family*, Vol. XVIII, No. 10 (1938), pp. 349–350; Francis H. McLean, "Opening the Door for the Aged," *The Family*, Vol. XIX, No. 1 (1938), pp. 25–27.

19. Stanley P. Davies, *Our Unchanging Goal: The Family*, Family Welfare Association of America, New York, 1938, p. 13.

20. Florence T. Waite, "New Emphases in Family Social Work," *The Family*, Vol. XVII, No. 5 (1936), p. 163.

21. Rudolph Danstedt, "How Are the New Membership Requirements Working Out?," *FWAA News Letter*, Vol. XIV, No. 1 (1939), p. 2.

IX. The War Years

FAMILY SOCIETIES EMERGED from the depression years with a clearer conception of purpose and program, a greater sense of unity, and a keen desire to study, analyze, and improve their services. The realignment of functions between public and private agencies made it possible for the family societies to devote more attention to developing techniques for helping families with problems of personal adjustment and family relationships. The strengthening of the casework program laid the groundwork for the many new counseling responsibilities that family agencies were to undertake as the nation moved into mobilization for defense and into World War II.

In the late thirties, the member agencies indicated that they wanted the Association to help them study several aspects of family agency programs: techniques of casework; staff development; research programs; the place of volunteers in family agencies, with emphasis on recruitment, training, and supervision; interpretation of family agency programs; the development of effective local boards. These were no ivory tower projects; their usefulness depended on their being a vital part of day-to-day agency operations, closely tied in with the potential contribution of family social work to family life.

There were other problems that called for the attention of national and local organizations. Although family societies no longer carried the responsibility for meeting economic need in their communities, there were many aspects of their relief function that had to be worked out, slowly and patiently, because of the still unsettled public relief situation. A survey of public relief in twenty-eight states, made by the American Association of Social Workers in the winter of 1938, showed mounting case loads, decreasing relief allowances, and the exhaustion of state and local funds for relief. In some states, restrictive eligibility legislation had been enacted and boards and staffs of local agencies tried—often with success—to get these laws repealed by gathering case material that showed the hardships inflicted on families and individuals by the rulings.

In view of the fact that appropriations rarely allowed even a minimum family budget, there was also continuing need for family societies to interpret to the general public the importance of adequate relief. A discussion of the problem, at a conference of representatives of large-city agencies in March, 1940, resulted in an agreement that the private agency should not accept direct responsibility to meet needs that a public agency relinquishes, because of lack of funds or by the adoption of arbitrary policies, except to demonstrate the effects of such limitations on family life. It was suggested that more conscious continuing study would help agencies determine to what extent they were really using relief in relation to the goals of family casework and what use families were making of relief given in these instances.

Like others undertaken by local agencies or sponsored by the Association, this discussion was based, in the approved charity organization tradition, on recorded experience. Analysis of family problems, and of methods of dealing with them, was undertaken at regional and other institutes, at agency staff meetings, and by several small groups of caseworkers from different agencies. One of these groups, brought together by the Association, used its discussions as the basis for two articles that were published in *The Family*.[1]

Cincinnati Associated Charities was one of the first agencies to emphasize family counseling as a function of a family society.[2] In 1939 this agency employed a part-time research worker to assist caseworkers in analyzing their own findings from their day-to-day work. In the Yearly Report for the agency, Anna Budd Ware wrote:

141

> It has long been our feeling that the greatest contribution to future understanding . . . will come, not from the theoretical writings of the more academic groups, but rather from the experience of those who are daily discussing and observing relationships and problems among hundreds of families. It is the material which will result from these studies which we hope to use as the basis of our next area of development—a more specific contribution to education for family life.[3]

In 1936 the Association appointed a Committee on Family and Marriage Counseling, with Mrs. Ware as chairman, to study and report on the nature and extent of family counseling under family social work and other auspices. Its report was presented to the Association Board in January, 1943.[4]

Local agencies continued to study a variety of questions related to casework practice. In what situations is it appropriate for the private agency to give relief?[5] Is a family agency equipped to serve an economically independent clientele? Is its work understood by the various groups in the community who might use the service or refer others to it? With what kinds of situations has the agency proved successful? How does it select from all those who come to it the individuals it can best serve? These agency studies were usually of a high order, showing candid self-scrutiny, ability to note progress without smugness, and to recognize flaws without disparaging self-criticism. There was no area of agency activity excluded from possible examination and the results, which were made available to the field through the Association, confirmed the conviction that, as Francis H. McLean pointed out, "continued evaluation and study are . . . the necessary concomitants of the work of every family agency. . . ."[6]

Such studies made by staff committees or by joint committees of staff and board, sometimes with the help of an outside consultant when the study was concerned with services to a special group, were important elements in staff development, as were the regional institutes and inter-city meetings. They did not, however, do much to increase the supply of competent workers. The recurring problem of finding enough qualified workers to fill staff vacancies was acute with most of the agencies and the situation was not improved by the decision of the Joint Vocational Service to cease operations in January, 1940. Both the Association and the member societies were convinced that the maintenance and development of personnel standards in family social work demanded a sound counseling and placement program. With the support of the Executive Committee and of the membership, Linton B. Swift, the Association's general director, called together representatives of other national organizations having an interest in personnel service in the casework field and together they worked out plans for a new placement agency. The Social Work Vocational Bureau, a nonprofit organization with a membership made up of social agencies and of social workers, began operations early in 1940. The following year Mabel Uzzell, who had been employed jointly by the Joint Vocational Service and the Association, came to the Association as full-time personnel director to counsel with member agencies on personnel, work-study plans, personnel classifications, employment practices, recruiting, and scholarship programs.

Another undertaking that greatly facilitated co-operation in the casework field on personnel and other matters of mutual concern was the Social Case Work Council of National Agencies, organized in 1940 by the Association and other national agencies as a section of the National Social Work Council, with Mr. Swift as chairman. The need for joint planning and action had become increasingly urgent with the development of the national defense program in the United States and the critical conditions in Europe.

Pre-War Period

The Association Board had early registered its abhorrence of the brutal policies of uprooting and disrupting families and persecuting people for their religious or political beliefs and had urged that refuge for as many as possible of the dispossessed be provided in this country. Many of the local societies, particularly the Jewish agencies, took an active part in organizing the community programs, in providing casework service for refugees, and in working with the United States Committee for the Care of European Children.

In 1940, with the passage of the Selective Service Act providing for compulsory military service, it became clear that further extension and adaptation of family agency and other casework services had to be planned. The Social Case Work Council of National Agencies, as one of its first jobs, assembled the experiences of the various national agencies on local problems resulting from mobilization efforts and formulated plans for providing casework service as needs emerged. A statement it prepared, "Social Aspects of the National Defense Program," was sent to all local agencies whose national organizations were members of the Council. The statement noted that "National morale in the Defense Program will be strong only as the morale of the individual is unshaken, and the morale of the men in the service will be impaired unless they are assured that a reasonable measure of security exists for their families and friends at home." [7] It emphasized the need for doing everything possible to conserve human values and outlined procedures for national and local planning to bring existing resources to bear where they were most needed.

The Association initiated a series of *Blue Bulletins* on "Family Welfare and the Home Front," the first of them suggesting ways in which family societies might give assistance to selective service boards in cases where deferment was requested because of dependency or where personal service to selectees and their families might be needed. The *Blue Bulletins* were continued over the next five years and served to keep the agencies informed 'of governmental regulations and other developments important to local programs.

The expansion and relocation of defense industries and the increase in work opportunities for both men and women brought their own problems. Men long unemployed found their wages garnisheed for debts contracted during the depression years. Others found that their particular skills did not meet the needs of defense industry and that their previous employment had closed down because of the priority given to defense efforts. As a result, even highly skilled workers sometimes could find nothing to do until they were retrained or new plants were opened. Such scarcity in the midst of plenty, so to speak, placed a great strain on family relations, which was made more difficult if the wife could get a job when her husband could not. A number of family agencies set up vocational guidance and employment counseling services—some with professionally trained vocational counselors, others with specially trained caseworkers as consultants—to help people not only in getting jobs but also in adjusting to them.

The migration of families to boom towns, with their overcrowd-

144

ing and lack of facilities for normal living—or the separation of families because the husband and father went alone to take a new job—gave rise to new problems or intensified old ones. The employment of mothers in defense industries called for increased facilities for the care of children. Some family societies expanded their homemaker service, although homemakers were difficult to get and proved to be an uneconomical method of providing for the care of children while the mothers worked, especially if the hours of work in industry were irregular.

National Planning

The entrance of the United States into the war in December, 1941, accentuated and complicated many of the existing strains on family life. The president of the Association, Laurence M. Williams of New Orleans, at once appointed a Committee on Family Welfare Program in the War and Postwar Period, with Stanley P. Davies, general director of the Community Service Society of New York, as chairman. The Committee reviewed and analyzed the new developments and related them to the basic program of family agencies. Family agency war-related activities showed a wide diversity, but the focus was on maintaining the values of family life. The Committee's report stressed that the "Continuity of normal services is our best insurance for the later meeting of post-war needs." [8]

The Association was represented on the Family Security Committee appointed by the Federal Security Agency in February, 1941, which was first concerned with the effect on families of the national defense program. It later considered ways of safeguarding families in a country at war. Helen Jeter, secretary of the Committee, pointed out:

> Family security is simply "family welfare" with the added implication that government has a responsibility to make family welfare secure in the interest of the national emergency. The problems of family security in wartime are those family agencies long have been facing during the series of human emergencies that contributed to the trend of developing social and economic relationships—the first world war, the post-war depression, the social disorganization during unprecedented prosperity, the long and bitter experience of industrial depression, the reception of refugees from Europe, family migration to find defense employment, finally war itself again. The problems as we have known

145

them under all these circumstances may include not only economic hardships, but emotional strains, maladjusted children, family separations, and the threat of mental breakdowns. . . .

The Family Security Committee has suggested that this is a time during which "the primary responsibility for family security and for co-ordination of community services lies with government, backed by the participation and support of voluntary effort." This Committee says further: "Regional, state, and local organization for defense purposes should provide for the co-ordination of all organized services for family security." This means that every voluntary or public family welfare agency in the country has a new responsibility for participation in community planning for wartime family security.[9]

Programs of Local Agencies

The new pressures on family life as the war advanced provided both an opportunity and a challenge to local family agencies. A number of the societies gave consultation service to mothers who wanted to take jobs in industry and tried to help them evaluate the pros and cons of such action and to give them information about resources for the care of their children. Casework service to day nurseries helped both the mothers and the day nursery personnel when problems arose in the children's adjustment or in connection with the mothers' work. The increased cost of living, income taxation, forced savings, and consumer rationing, requiring greater family discipline and care in management, brought new clients to the family society for help in budget planning.

The public agencies gradually assumed responsibility for dependency investigations for the selective service boards and the private agencies undertook to give personal service to selectees and their families. They were particularly concerned with the men who were rejected for reasons of physical or emotional health and, later, the men discharged as unfit soon after induction. Far too many of these men owed their disabilities to physical privations and emotional tensions suffered during the years of the depression. The breakup of families due to separation, the tensions and anxieties arising from the war, the hasty, often impulsive, marriages of young men about to be inducted into the armed forces, called for skilled casework service in helping husbands and wives work out their problems. For the most part, these were families not in need of economic help and a few of the societies, notably the Jewish family

146

agency in New York, offered marriage or family counseling on a fee basis so as to reach the middle-income group who would prefer to pay for service. Special efforts were also made by many of the agencies to interpret family casework services to men and women in industry—to employers and to union stewards—so that employees might find help for family troubles that were interfering with their work, causing the much publicized absenteeism, and slowing down production.

Association Activities

For these and similar projects, some of them frankly experimental, the Association gave suggestions through the *Blue Bulletins*, through reports of special committees, and through other publications, as well as through gathering and distributing detailed accounts of current experiences. The *Blue Bulletins* also carried essential material about the changing community scene that was affecting both family societies and the families they served. The material included co-ordination of social programs; agreements reached with the American Red Cross and other war relief agencies on division of work; and interpretation of governmental regulations, such as rationing of gasoline and other commodities, salary stabilization, job freeze orders, and so on.

The Association's maintenance of close working relationships with other national agencies, individually and through the National Social Work Council, and with federal agencies such as the Office of Defense Health and Welfare Services, the War Manpower Commission, Children's Bureau, Office of Education, Veterans Administration, and others, were of great benefit to the whole family social work movement. Linton B. Swift, the general director, and Ralph A. Uihlein, the president of the Association, both served on the Advisory Committee on Social Welfare, Mr. Uihlein as chairman. This Committee, under Charles P. Taft of the Office of Defense Health and Welfare Services, met monthly to advise informally on welfare activities related to defense. Largely as a result of this Committee's efforts, the War Manpower Commission included "welfare services to civilians" in its list of essential activities, thus providing a safeguard against the raiding of social agency personnel by industry. Nevertheless, agencies lost many of their workers: some were drafted into the armed forces and others took employment with the Red Cross and other war-related services. Some social workers had been attached to clinical units in Army Replacement Training Centers early in the war, but it was not until 1943 that the army established an official classification (army serial specification number 263) for social workers, which made it possible for inducted social workers to be assigned to social work jobs.

The loss of family agency staff members, together with the acute personnel shortage in the social work field, began to make itself felt early in 1942, at the time when the demand for extension of services to new groups was steadily growing. In November, 1941, the Association had appointed a Committee on Family Social Work Personnel, which recognized that there was need for an active program of recruitment and training for social work if agency services were to be safeguarded. As agency staff vacancies continued to mount and replacements with qualified staff became increasingly difficult, the Committee proposed a work-study plan that was put into effect by many local societies. This plan provided for full professional education in an accredited school of social work for staff members who worked in the agency part time; the work-study program usually took three, rather than two, years, to qualify for the master's degree. The Committee later drew up material on personnel practices, job classifications, and salary scales, which was of great value to local agencies in establishing and maintaining standards.

As the war advanced, the Association received a number of requests for consultation from new or suddenly expanded industrial centers—towns or villages that had become cities overnight and lacked facilities to take care of the new population—as well as from established industrial communities facing new problems. Other national agencies were also receiving similar requests and they, like the Association, did not have staff or funds to take on the additional work. In May, 1943, the American War-Community Services was established to help these hard-pressed communities develop needed services. The new agency was a co-operative venture of six national agencies: Family Welfare Association of America; American Federation of International Institutes; Child Welfare League of America;

148

National Board of the Young Women's Christian Association; National Organization for Public Health Nursing; and National Urban League. It was financed by Community Chests, for the purpose of providing the much-needed additional field service.

A Service Co-operation Committee, made up of representatives from the six national agencies and consultants from Community Chests and Councils, American Federation of Labor, Congress of Industrial Organizations, National Social Work Council, and the Office of Community War Services of the Federal Security Agency, met monthly to consider problems of inter-agency co-operation and of strategy for local community service. Thus it was possible to have a continuing interchange of information about conditions and needs of war-affected communities and clearance between national agencies and local social planning groups. The plan helped to eliminate conflicts and duplications in field service and to facilitate unity in planning, both nationally and locally.

The emphasis of AWCS was on the study of the needs and resources of each community and on finding local leaders who would join the field workers in planning a well-rounded program that would be supported financially and otherwise by local groups. In a number of instances, field workers from two or more of the agencies participating in AWCS visited a community simultaneously, and conferred jointly with local groups. In addition to giving direct service to hard-pressed communities, the staff of AWCS participated in collecting data on such subjects as veterans' problems, industrial counseling, manpower regulations, day-care needs, and housing, which was useful to all family societies. Lack of funds made it necessary to terminate AWCS in December, 1947. The regular staff of the Association absorbed as much as possible of the service still needed by the communities. The National Social Welfare Assembly (formerly the National Social Work Council) accepted responsibility for carrying, on a voluntary basis, the co-ordinating functions of the Service Co-operation Committee.

Publications

The Publications Service of the Association also keyed much of its program to war-related services, without losing sight of the long-time programs of family social work. Articles in *The Family* described the work done by social workers at army rehabilitation centers, at hospitals with ill and disabled servicemen, and counseling service in day nurseries, as well as technical articles on marriage counseling and the use of psychiatric consultants. Articles from London and Canada described methods of meeting war conditions in those countries.

In May of 1938 the Association appointed a preliminary publications committee, with Betsey Libbey of Philadelphia as chairman, to give general consideration to the organization's publishing program. It recommended that a Committee on Association Publications Program be set up to undertake a detailed review of the Association's periodicals and other publications.

In the summer of 1939 this new committee was appointed, with Cora Kasius, of the New York Community Service Society, as chairman. The Committee reviewed the minutes and report of the preliminary committee and held several meetings that fall. It recognized the need for expanding the *News Letter* in order to carry additional material on administrative and organizational matters of particular concern to board members. It also believed that *The Family* should indicate by its title the chief purpose this journal had always served and for which it had originally been intended— that of providing a medium through which caseworkers in all fields could exchange experience.

In its report in November, 1939, the Committee recommended that a new periodical, to be called *Highlights,* should replace the *News Letter.* This recommendation was accepted and the first issue of *Highlights* was published in March, 1940. (Its name was changed to *Family Service Highlights* in 1952.) The Committee also recommended that *The Family* carry a subtitle, *Journal of Social Case Work,* which should later become the official title of *The Family.* (In 1946 the name was changed to *Journal of Social Casework,* and in 1950 the title became *Social Casework.*) [10]

The Publications Committee also recommended that an Editorial Advisory Committee to *The Family* be appointed (there had been one in the early days of the journal) and that the Association expand its services in making available, in pamphlet and book form, materials related both to Association activities and to casework developments in all fields of practice.

Some of the books and pamphlets issued by the Association during this period were: *Psychiatric Aspects of Civilian Morale;* [11] *A Guidebook for Beginners in Public Assistance Work;* [12] and *Family Budget Counseling.* [13] *Interviewing: Its Principles and Methods,* [14] by Annette Garrett of the Smith College School for Social Work, was widely used not only by social workers but by other groups as well. Two publications were results of studies of the war-stimulated field of industrial counseling; one a pamphlet, *Counseling Services for Industrial Workers* [15] by Mary Palevsky, a member of the AWCS staff; the other a book, *Counseling Methods for Personnel Workers* [16] by Annette Garrett. In 1939 *Social Case Work in Practice—Six Case Studies,* [17] by Florence Hollis, was published, and soon became a standard textbook in casework courses. The case record exhibit and the mimeographed case records issued by the Association also provided valuable teaching material for agencies and schools of social work.

Organizational Committees

A by-product of AWCS which was of value to the field as a whole was its experimentation, facilitated by joint field visits, with the idea of combining two or more services under one organization when such an arrangement was in the best interests of a given community. Such combinations had been practical necessities in the early days of charity organization and in the later 1930's. There was a revival of interest in mergers since combined service seemed to be more efficient and economical than separate agencies with closely related functions. Between 1934 and 1944 there were sixty mergers of family societies with other casework agencies—the majority with children's agencies. Most of these mergers resulted in improved casework programs for the communities involved, but others were less successful, largely because of hurried and inadequate planning.

The Association appointed a Committee on Relations within the Social Casework Field, which gave careful study to the question of combining services. Its report (December, 1944) outlined principles and procedures for safeguarding the integrity of agency services and for assuring maximum benefit to clients if a merger was contemplated.

Other committees made significant contributions to the planning

151

and programming of both local agencies and the Association. A Committee on Association Membership Participation recommended in 1942 that each society should have not one, as heretofore, but three voting representatives at meetings of Association membership. The Committee proposed the establishment of a General Assembly, composed of the executive, a board member, and a member of the professional staff of each member society (the last from agencies with two or more on the staff besides the executive), which would meet regularly every two years and on call of the Board as needed at other times. The Committee's recommendations were adopted in 1943 and the first meeting of the General Assembly was held in May, 1944. Another step toward furthering closer working relationships between the membership and the national body was the arrangement for the chairmen of the Regional Committees to serve ex officio on the Association Board.

A special committee was appointed to consider financial support of the Association, another area where more active participation by the membership was needed. The charter members had planned that the Association would get its income from membership dues of ten dollars a year plus contributions raised by the agencies, the amounts depending on the size of the community. In 1919 a special appropriation from the Russell Sage Foundation had made it possible to expand the Association program, but the grant was made with the understanding that the membership would assume full financial responsibility as quickly as possible. In 1920 the societies accepted a "quota" plan of dues (2 per cent of the service budget), but very few of the societies met the full obligation and the Russell Sage Foundation continued its grants until 1950. There was gradual improvement in payment of agency dues but many failed to meet the agreed-on quota and, in 1940, the Committee on Support of Family Social Work recommended a graduated series of steps to bring the payments of all members up to the full dues level. In 1943 this plan was made mandatory, the steps to be completed within a five-year period. Some modifications in the dues formula were adopted by the General Assembly in 1947. The principle of self-support so strongly expressed in 1911 was on its way to realization in practice.

Throughout the war years the emphasis in both national and

local planning for family service had been on integrating wartime activities with the continuing program of family social work. The idea expressed earlier by the Committee on Family Welfare Program in the War and Postwar Period, that "continuity of normal services is our best insurance for the later meeting of post-war needs," was echoed by one of the local societies: ". . . whatever our function and role is in the national emergency [it] should be studiously geared to what we can visualize as the needs and, therefore, the role of family agencies when this present crisis is past and when we perhaps will face what may be a more trying and perplexing situation." [18] The activities undertaken by the societies to meet needs brought on by war conditions, whether in day care consultation, family counseling, or in relation to workers in industry, was an adaptation of their normal casework service.

During the war years, the Association maintained its usual activities and, like the local agencies, reached out to new groups, through AWCS, through the *Blue Bulletins* (sent to a mailing list of about fifteen hundred) and the expanded publications program, and through contacts with governmental and national voluntary agencies. It re-established its Personnel Service on a stronger basis and set up a plan for a General Assembly in order to facilitate membership participation in Association affairs.

References

1. "Aspects of Relations with the Community in Family Casework: Part 1, Some Protective Aspects of Family Case Work," *The Family*, Vol. XX, No. 2 (1939), pp. 35–41; "Part 2, Our Relationship to the Community as Seen Through Referrals," Vol. XX, No. 3 (1939), pp. 80–86.

2. Dr. Julien E. Benjamin, "Family Consultation Service as a Function of a Family Agency," *Family Life and National Recovery*, Family Welfare Association of America, New York, 1935.

3. "Digging for Facts," *Highlights*, Family Welfare Association of America, Vol. I, No. 2 (1940), pp. 25–26.

4. "FWAA Board Meets in January," *Highlights*, FWAA, Vol. III, No. 10 (1943), p. 158.

5. Cora Kasius (ed.), *Relief Practice in a Family Agency*, Family Welfare Association of America, New York, 1942.

6. Francis H. McLean, *Surveys in the Family Field*, Family Welfare Association of America, New York, 1939; also in *The Family*, Vol. XX, No. 4 (1939), p. 115.

7. *Social Aspects of the National Defense Program*, Social Case Work Council of National Agencies, New York, 1940, p. 1.

8. *Preliminary Report, Committee on Family Welfare Program in the War and Post-War Period,* Family Welfare Association of America, New York, 1942, p. 4.

9. Helen R. Jeter, "Wartime Problems of Family Security," *The Family,* Vol. XXIII, No. 3 (1942), pp. 83, 91.

10. Cora Kasius, "Searching for Unwritten Manuscripts," *Highlights,* FWAA, Vol. 1, No. 10 (1941), pp. 158–159.

11. *Psychiatric Aspects of Civilian Morale,* Prepared by the Military Mobilization Committee of the American Psychiatric Association, Family Welfare Association of America, New York, 1942.

12. Ella Lee Cowgill, *A Guidebook for Beginners in Public Assistance Work,* Family Welfare Association of America, New York, 1940.

13. Dorothy L. Book (ed.), *Family Budget Counseling,* Family Welfare Association of America, New York, 1944.

14. Annette Garrett, *Interviewing: Its Principles and Methods,* Family Welfare Association of America, New York, 1942.

15. Mary Palevsky, *Counseling Services for Industrial Workers,* Family Welfare Association of America, New York, 1945.

16. Annette Garrett, *Counseling Methods for Personnel Workers,* Family Welfare Association of America, New York, 1945.

17. Florence Hollis, *Social Case Work in Practice—Six Case Studies,* Family Welfare Association of America, New York, 1939.

18. "Highlights Across the Country," *Highlights,* FWAA, Vol. II, No. 9 (1942), p. 133.

X. Postwar Period

In 1945 FAMILY social workers everywhere were saddened by the death of Francis H. McLean, who had been part of the Association since 1911 and had done much to shape its philosophy and program. The following year the death of Linton B. Swift, whose strong and devoted leadership had guided the Association and the membership for over twenty years, created another serious loss for the Association.

It was fortunate that both Mr. McLean and Mr. Swift shared the basic philosophy that had infused the Association from its inception. Both men saw their work and the day-to-day work of the Association and the member societies not only related to immediate needs but as building for the future. Mr. McLean once said:

> I like to think of the adventures of this winter not just as a joint exploration of our member agencies in a certain limited geographical area, with the Association looking on, advising, encouraging. Rather it has been, and I think should continue to be, a real going along together in which the Association itself is but one of the companions on the trail. Field relationships, like relationships of client and case worker, must be constantly responding to the changing needs and possibilities of this changing period. Like casework relationships, they are capable of a high degree of diversification, and the extent to which this diversification is developed is essential to their continuing usefulness. . . . The ways ahead are many, the trails of exploration are

155

infinitely varied, new methods of working together must develop to meet the challenge of the dazzling vistas before us.[1]

The same point of view about the basic aims and philosophy of family social work was expressed by Mr. Swift:

Implicit in that philosophy there are certain concepts which, although not always definitely expressed, have meant an emphasis upon growth rather than upon fixed standards of work; upon the substance rather than the form; upon the people who are doing the job rather than the organization through which it is done; upon the value of differences between people and communities rather than upon any imposed uniformity. In each of these pairs of concepts, the second has a value based solely upon the extent to which it expresses the dynamics of the first. . . . [This philosophy] has meant a growth based upon expressions of local needs rather than upon the conceptions of any one central group. It has meant a national organization deriving its existence from independent local agencies, as distinguished from a system of local branches or units established upon the authority of a national agency. . . . It has meant an Association which keeps close to trends within its membership, rather than a national agency which attempts authoritatively to direct such trends.[2]

Much as the staff, board, and membership mourned the loss of these old friends, they faced the necessity for carrying on the work without them. On June 7, 1946, the Board announced the appointment of Frank J. Hertel as general director. He had formerly been head of the Family Welfare Association of Minneapolis and had been director of the Association's Field Service since 1944.

Committee on Current and Future Planning

It was in keeping with the convictions of Linton Swift and Francis McLean that in 1943, when pressures of war conditions were at their height, the Association appointed a Committee on Current and Future Planning, with Malcolm S. Nichols of the Boston Family Welfare Society as chairman, to review the program and to identify unmet needs. The Committee's report was ready for the 1946 Biennial Meeting, the first to be held after the war. Many of the findings and suggestions of the Committee were paralleled in the discussions at the Biennial sessions. In both there was emphasis on the prevention of family disorganization and breakdown as the basic reason for the existence of the family agency and both stressed the importance of casework service in the treatment of marital problems, in helping the returning veteran re-orient himself to life as a civilian, in recognizing and interpreting the needs of the older person as an individual.

The Committee also commented on the development of fee pay-ment, which by 1945 had been established in fifteen agencies. The report stated: "In the judgment of the Committee . . . the charging of fees is a sound development. First, the principle of paying for goods or services is an integral part of our American culture. Second, family casework, as a method of helping families with personal difficulties, is available only within the setting of the family agency, and, therefore, it is neither sound nor just to dis-criminate against those willing and able to pay and who would not feel free to use the service unless given the opportunity to pay." [3] Other advantages of fee payment for service have subse-quently been noted: its value in interpreting casework to the com-munity; its positive psychological effect on the client; and its usefulness in extending service to new groups.

Marriage counseling, the Committee recognized, had become an accepted and undifferentiated part of the programs of many family societies. It noted:

> Such counseling, which includes requests for information about marital relationships, helps in reaching a decision around the question of whether or not to live together as marriage partners, assistance in evaluating the effects of a wife's employment on family relationships, consultation concerning sexual maladjustment, and so on, is a kind of service which should be part and parcel of the work of a family agency, and should include pre-marital as well as post-marital counseling. . . . In the opin-ion of the Committee . . . it is not logical to separate marriage coun-seling from other types of family counseling. Many of the same families that have difficulties in marriage also need help in their adjustment in other areas . . . the problem of parent-child relationships . . . health problems, vocational problems, and others are likewise closely related and it is not practical to try to divide the counseling process among several different agencies.[4]

Although the Committee felt that casework service to individuals and families should continue to be the major focus of the family agency, it pointed out that there was also a pressing need for family social work to move on into the area of family life education in order to prevent social and family breakdown. Miss Richmond, in her paper at the fiftieth anniversary celebration in Buffalo in 1927, had seen such a possibility, analogous to public health education, focused on the conservation of health rather than on the cure of disease. At that same meeting Dr. Ernest R. Groves had suggested "experimentation along this line by the more progressive family welfare agencies." [5] The Committee on Current and Future Planning believed that leadership in a program of family life education should be an integral part of the responsibility of family societies, a point of view strongly endorsed at the 1946 Biennial Meeting.

During the course of its assignment, the Committee considered the advisability of a common title for national and local family social work organizations and finally recommended "Family Service," which was approved by the membership in a mail vote, and in 1946 the national organization changed its name to the Family Service Association of America. A sizable number of the member societies also incorporated the key words "Family Service" in their titles, thus re-emphasizing their common purposes.

The Committee outlined several legitimate and desirable functions of the family service agency: the prevention of family disorganization; the provision of casework service for troubled men and women; experimentation with new ways of helping people; and the improvement of social conditions. The Committee, however, believed that "few, if any, agencies today [1946] are completely equipped to discharge fully what is implied in this . . . program. This wide and deep gap between desirable program and the availability of experienced personnel leads the Committee to recommend strong concentration upon agency provisions for staff development, both local and national planning in recruiting for professional education in social work and [in improvement of] personnel practices, including adequate salaries. . . ." [6]

Personnel Committee

Personnel shortage, which had been a serious problem during the war, became even more acute as a result of the expansion of casework programs to meet postwar needs, including international social services. Also, new family agencies, some started by American War-Community Services, and new demands for casework service by a number of organizations accentuated the shortage. The Association's Personnel Committee was preparing statements on principles of personnel practices, on suggested salary scales, and on job qualifications. Many agencies continued the work-study programs started during the war, and in addition the Personnel Committee gave practical suggestions for scholarship programs.

In 1946, local agency budget appropriations for scholarships totaled $120,000, as against $74,000 three years earlier. The personnel director of the Association undertook to interview social workers released from the armed forces and candidates who applied for help in getting professional training. Later the Association, in conjunction with the Social Work Vocational Bureau and other national agencies, participated in promoting the expansion of public employment services to the social work field as a help in recruitment as well as in placement. Opportunities for further professional development of workers already on the job came, as always, from regional institutes and round tables, and a number of agencies had regular staff seminars on casework and supervision. Psychiatric consultants often served as leaders of seminars and contributed greatly to staff development.

Program Emphases

In spite of staff shortages, many agencies expanded their services. Some developed, either within the agency or in the community, special resources for older people, such as more adequate institutional care, boarding homes, group living arrangements, clubs and recreational programs. Some developed homemaker service to provide care for the older client during an interim period until an appropriate plan could be worked out. Others maintained a special group of homemakers to be used only for this group. The Family Service Society of Hartford, Connecticut, sponsored an experiment in counseling and community organization to meet the needs of older persons. This project was financed by a foundation and was an integral part of the society's work.[7]

Industrial counseling, which had received special attention during the war, was continued, and in addition a number of local agencies played an active part in the training courses for union counselors planned by the CIO, usually in co-operation with local councils

159

of social agencies. Family societies also took part in programs for the care of newcomers to this country—war brides and displaced persons who had been in concentration camps.

Interest was expressed by a number of agencies in having the Association establish a committee, composed of professional persons, to study the likenesses and differences in philosophy and method of the two orientations in casework. At its meeting on June 6, 1947, the Board approved the appointment of a Committee to Study Basic Concepts in Casework Practice. Eleanor P. Sheldon, director of Family and Children's Services of Stamford, Connecticut, served as chairman.

The report of this Committee was presented to the Board in June, 1950, and published by the Association under the title, *A Comparison of Diagnostic and Functional Casework Concepts*.[8] It included statements of principles underlying the practice in both casework orientations, as well as illustrative cases. This publication received wide distribution and undoubtedly served to clarify much existing confusion. It stimulated the writing of several other articles and reports, including a book prepared by staff members of Jewish Family Service of New York and published by the Association.[9]

Committee on Family Life Education

For several years caseworkers in a number of agencies had engaged in informal education activities with groups of parents or adolescents. Later, in line with the suggestion of the Committee on Current and Future Planning, these activities in family life education increased. At the 1948 Biennial Meeting held in Detroit, a session was devoted to reports by agencies of what they had been doing and of the problems they had encountered. It was obvious that there was need to reach a definitive understanding of the family agency's role in family life education if it was to become an effective service in the prevention of family breakdown and the strengthening of family life.

In 1948, the Association appointed a Committee on Family Life Education, with Mrs. Grace C. Mayberg of Minneapolis as chairman. Its charge was "to define the nature and place of family life education in the program of family service agencies; examine the content and objectives of current projects in family services agencies;

consider the relationship of such activities in the family field to those in allied fields; suggest what skills are required to carry on a program of family life education in a family service agency; suggest to family agencies certain guides and principles that are essential to the development of a sound program of family life education." [10]

The Committee reported that in 1948 eighty-one agencies had participated to some extent in programs of family life education. There was agreement that:

> [family life education] is an extension of the function of the family agency in that it makes available to groups information that is in everyday use by the family caseworker in service to individuals. It is not a substitute for individualized casework. . . . While it may emerge as a third function of family agencies, the Committee recommends further experimentation at the practice level before the field as a whole formally calls for its adoption and implementation. Family agencies should embark on a program of family life education only when their casework program is on a solid footing. Casework remains the core of family agency program and family life education should be regarded distinctly as an additional service. [11]

Extension of Association Services

The demand for Association leadership in research and interpretation had been recurrent over the years. Some local agencies did excellent work in interpretation, a few had undertaken research, but both local societies and the Association were handicapped by lack of funds to employ special staff. As one step toward meeting the need for interpretation, the Association engaged a public relations consultant during the war years and in 1947 was able to establish its Public Relations Service, with a Public Relations Committee, to advise the local societies and to prepare material that could be used both locally and nationally.

Public Relations Service soon developed a variety of projects on the national level; it gave consultative service to feature writers which resulted in the publication of some excellent articles in national magazines on family life and family problems. The response to these articles showed how great the need was for skilled service in personal and family problems and how many communities still had no such service available. This program spurred the trend toward identification of national and locals under the name

161

"Family Service," stimulated public relations programs at the local community level, and both directly and indirectly strengthened the interest of local and national board members in the movement as a whole.

Research was recognized as a valuable adjunct to intelligent interpretation of services and to useful comparisons of activities of different agencies, as well as an essential means for studying methods and agency programs. Information Service, which was earlier known as the Department of Studies and Information, with its Committee on Statistics and Studies, had made a beginning in gathering materials on the function, organization, and activities of the family field through the yearly reports from the agencies. The materials included studies undertaken by member agencies, which were made available to others with similar interests.

In 1945, the Association engaged a research consultant whose responsibility, along with other assignments, was to take over the compilation of family casework statistics, a task the Russell Sage Foundation was about to relinquish after having carried it for twenty years. Working with the Committee on Statistics and Studies, the research consultant developed a pamphlet, *Guides to Agency Research*,[12] and helped individual societies with advice on studies covering a wide range of subjects directly related to current activities and planning. The continuing need for additional staff to carry on operational research, such as studies of multifunctional agencies, and research directly related to American family living— problems of the aging, of marital difficulty, of child rearing—was not lost sight of but could not be undertaken with available personnel.

At its meeting in December, 1945, the Board of the Association approved the recommendation of the Membership Committee for a pre-member affiliate relationship plan for family agencies interested in working toward membership in the Association. The time limit placed on this relationship was three years, with no more than fifteen to twenty agencies to be in the plan at any one time.[13]

In the years immediately following the end of the second world war, there was a marked increase in the number of communities asking Association help in establishing family societies. The increase was due in part to the work of the AWCS, which had touched many communities hitherto unaware of family service, and in part

162

to the extended use of casework during the war, together with the generally favorable response to interpretation of family service.

Also, most agencies reported an increase in requests for help with personal problems and a decrease in calls for economic help, although the high cost of living, due to inflation, and, in 1949, an aggravation of family problems because of rising unemployment and economic dislocation, were important factors in family situations. Both the Association and most of the local agencies were understaffed, but there was some slight improvement in the personnel situation as a whole. Salaries had been increased, staff turnover was slightly lower, and there were fewer vacancies. These, plus dynamic growth in thinking and in practice, made it possible for many agencies to offer more and better services and the outlook for continued development was optimistic.

Impact of War in Korea

The war in Korea had its inevitable repercussions on families and on the services of family agencies. Military mobilization affected not only the individual and his family but the community; industrial mobilization, like military mobilization, meant separation of families, migration of workers to new or expanded defense communities, disruption of the home through the employment of mothers—all contributing to a mounting sense of tension and uncertainty about the future. As Charlotte Towle pointed out at the 1950 Biennial Meeting, held in New York City, "Reinforcing family security is not a new responsibility for social work. Social work has always served families whose individual worlds have been stressful. The noteworthy features today are the totality of life's uncertainty and the fact that parents and children have grown up during precarious times—war, inflation, depression, war, inflation, and now a defense economy. . . . Many . . . are vulnerable by reason of longstanding strain . . . stresses become more traumatic through repetition." [14]

The reports made by the Association's six Regional Committees during this period gave a vivid picture of the impact of defense mobilization as seen by family agencies the country over. New industries were springing up overnight, with the result that what recently was a "village crossroad" had become an industrial city.

163

Urban areas in which defense-related industries were located reported greatly increased employment and, at the same time, considerable unemployment was prevalent in non-defense industries that could not secure priorities on basic materials. A large number of women took employment in industry; two other groups also were drawn into the labor force—older workers whose skills were still in demand and handicapped persons whose abilities fitted them for certain types of jobs. Within the short space of two weeks, 124 new areas had been designated as critical by the Office of Defense Mobilization and the Housing and Home Finance Agency. Some of these communities had no hospitals, no sewage system, and totally inadequate housing. Housing, day care for children, and recreation were the needs most frequently mentioned by the Regional Committees.

As for the family agencies, the Regional Committees found that more people were asking for help with problems of budgeting or of indebtedness directly related to the rising cost of living. Problems of behavior, which had been thought to be related to the tension of World War II, now seemed to be part of the general pattern of living. Parent-child tensions, marital friction, and unmarried parenthood were paramount among the problems with which families were asking for casework service. In some communities, the unavailability of public assistance for unemployed workers brought new demands on private agencies to meet basic financial needs. In addition, there was pressure on the family societies, hard pushed though they were by staff shortages and insufficient funds, to extend their services to nearby uncovered areas. There was need for planning on all levels—local, state, and national—if social services were to keep pace with the demands made upon them.

To meet the needs of families in defense communities the Association joined with fourteen other national agencies in the formation of the United Community Defense Services, a project financed by the United Defense Fund. The Association began its work in this joint effort in April, 1952, establishing a separate unit with three field consultants. The first job of the field consultants was to understand the individual community situation and to enlist the interest of local leaders in developing plans. In general, the UCDS staff of the Association undertook to give service to these hard-pressed communities in much the same way as had the AWCS ten years earlier.

The Association was represented on the National Committee on Social Work in Defense Mobilization and took an active part in efforts to define the role of social workers in the armed forces and to obtain maximum use of their skills in both the armed forces and in relation to defense activities.[15] Particular emphasis was placed on establishing selected social work positions as "critical civilian occupations" and helping qualified workers find the jobs where their skills were most needed rather than responding to the frequent and inevitable emergency situations. As Charlotte Towle pointed out, "Through past experience we have some criteria to guide us in determining where and under what circumstances we [social workers] can serve effectively." [16]

In addition to taking part in projects related to war and defense, the Association represented the membership with those national agencies whose activities affected family social work, directly or indirectly. By 1950 this had become a complex and many-sided task, owing to the increase in the number of governmental agencies and of voluntary national associations in many areas of social work. Board and staff members of the Association served on numerous committees set up by the federal government and by the National Social Welfare Assembly not only to interpret the needs of families but to mobilize the influence of the family service field in support of a broad national program to improve social services in communities that were poorly served and to foster team play in meeting family and community needs.

The Association staff took part in such national meetings in Washington, D. C., as the National Conference on Prevention and Control of Juvenile Delinquency, called by the Attorney General's office in 1946; the National Conference on Family Life in 1948; and the Midcentury White House Conference on Children and Youth, in 1950. Other working relationships on the national level were of both immediate and long-range value to local agencies, such as participation in the Social Work Vocational Bureau, the National Council on Social Work Education, the Commission on Marriage and the Home of the American Bar Association, the International Congress of Mental Health, and the International Conference of Social Work.

Responsibility for Social Planning

The Association Committee on Current and Future Planning had reaffirmed the primary functions of family service societies—casework service to individuals and families and community leadership in the improvement of living conditions directly affecting family life—and went on to say:

> In spite of this acknowledged contribution toward . . . social change, it is nevertheless true that the casework function of the family agency, in terms of both pace and emphasis, has developed more rapidly than its community leadership function. Few agencies make ample, if any, budget provision to implement this . . . part of their program and yet community leadership . . . must be based upon careful research and fact finding followed by adequate provisions for public interpretation and education. Greater emphasis needs to be given to this obligation now and in the future if the two major functions of the family service agency are to develop hand in hand.[17]

Questions about the effectiveness of the family field, both locally and nationally, in working for the improvement of social conditions continued to be raised. In 1950, Robert F. Nelson, executive director of the United Charities of Chicago, suggested that reasons for the failure of some family societies to take responsibility for the improvement of living conditions might be related to the lack of guiding principles. He offered a few that he thought might clarify the place and conduct of the family society in the field of social action: "The family agency . . . has an obligation to be alert to conditions beyond individual control . . . to ascertain the possible extent of their influences on all families. . . . the place of the agency in social action should be determined by the testimony that comes from casework process, rather than on conviction lacking a base in agency practice. . . . action should be predicated on formal authority of the board." [18]

At its meeting in June, 1950, the Board of the Association authorized the appointment of a Committee on Association Social Policy, to be composed of both professional and lay members. This Committee, which was under the chairmanship of Mrs. Malcolm J. Edgerton, was asked to develop a statement of social policy for the family field as a guide to national, state, and local action on matters affecting the security and stability of the family, and to present its report to the General Assembly at the Biennial Meeting scheduled to take place in Buffalo in November, 1952.

166

Study of Scope and Methods

In June, 1950, the Board also authorized the appointment of a Committee on Methods and Scope, which was given the assignment of examining trends in casework practice and of making recommendations about the scope, focus, and direction of family agency programs. Such an appraisal of program and methods seemed indicated both because of uncertainty among caseworkers about treatment techniques appropriate to work in a family agency and because of the seeming lack of focus of agency programs in view of the many types of services they were providing.

The Committee, under the chairmanship of Rae Carp Weil of the Jewish Family Service Association of Cleveland, submitted its report to the Board in May, 1953, and the Board approved its release. It was subsequently published by the Association under the title *Scope and Methods of the Family Service Agency*.[19] This pamphlet received wide attention and was used extensively by both lay and professional groups.

In defining the scope of a family agency, the Committee reaffirmed the two traditional major functions: providing casework services and participating in community planning. It listed for the first time three secondary functions: conducting group educational activities; contributing to professional education; and engaging in research.

The Committee noted that these latter three activities had been an integral part of many agencies for a number of years, and therefore were not new. "Some agencies may include all three of these secondary functions . . . and some none; others may include one or more for a limited period of time on a planned basis. These secondary functions grow out of, and are dependent upon, the two major functions—chiefly the casework program." [20]

The Committee described the general purposes and principles of social casework and identified two treatment aims: (1) treatment aimed at maintaining adaptive patterns and (2) treatment aimed at modification of adaptive patterns.

In its conclusion, the Committee pointed out that the report was not submitted as a blueprint but was intended as a guide for agencies in developing their particular programs. It stressed that "variations in program development and differences in emphases

167

are to be expected and encouraged. Family agency programs, by principle and tradition, have always been flexible and have been adapted to meet changing conditions. In the same way, agencies have been creative and experimental in developing new techniques and services, incorporating and applying new knowledge about human relationships as it has become available." [21]

References

1. Francis H. McLean, "Adventures in Field Relationships," *New Perspectives in Family Social Work,* Family Welfare Association of America Report for 1933 and 1934, p. 11.
2. Linton B. Swift, *Unity in Diversity*, FWAA Report for 1931 and 1932, pp. 7–8.
3. "Report of the Committee on Current and Future Planning," Family Service Association of America, New York, 1946, p. 8.
4. *Ibid.,* pp. 14–15.
5. Ernest R. Groves, "Education for Family Life," *Family Life Today,* ed. Margaret E. Rich, Houghton Mifflin Company, Boston, 1928, p. 57.
6. "Report of the Committee on Current and Future Planning" (*supra*), p. 6.
7. Ruth Hill, "Focusing Attention on Older People's Needs," *Journal of Social Casework,* Vol. XXX, No. 10 (1949), pp. 405–411.
8. Cora Kasius (ed.), *A Comparison of Diagnostic and Functional Casework Concepts,* Report of the Committee to Study Basic Concepts in Casework Practice, Family Service Association of America, New York, 1950.
9. M. Robert Gomberg and Frances T. Levinson (eds.), *Diagnosis and Process in Family Counseling—Evolving Concepts through Practice*, Family Service Association of America, New York, 1951.
10. "Family Life Education," *Highlights,* Family Service Association of America, Vol. XII, No. 5 (1951), p. 66.
11. *Ibid.,* pp. 73–74.
12. *Guides to Agency Research,* Report of the Sub-Committee on Agency Research, Committee on Statistics and Studies, Family Service Association of America, New York, 1950.
13. "FWAA Board Meeting," *Highlights,* Family Welfare Association of America, Vol. VI, No. 9 (1946), p. 146; also "Pre-Member Affiliate Relationship for Family Agencies," *Highlights,* FWAA, Vol. VII, No. 2 (1946), pp. 24–26.
14. Charlotte Towle, "Reinforcing Family Security Today," *Social Casework,* Vol. XXXII, No. 2 (1951), p. 57.
15. Frank J. Hertel, "Family Service at Midcentury," *Highlights,* FSAA, Vol. XII, No. 2 (1951), p. 26.
16. Towle, *op. cit.,* p. 59.
17. "Report of the Committee on Current and Future Planning" (*supra*), p. 2.
18. Robert F. Nelson, "Suggested Principles for Social Action in the Family Agency," *Highlights,* FSAA, Vol. XI, No. 10 (1950), pp. 146–147.
19. *Scope and Methods of the Family Service Agency,* Report of the Committee on Methods and Scope, Family Service Association of America, New York, 1953.
20. *Ibid.,* p. 3.
21. *Ibid.,* pp. 21–22.

XI. The Present

In November, 1952, the Association held its Biennial Meeting in Buffalo, joining with the Buffalo Family Service Society in celebrating the seventy-fifth anniversary of the founding of the first charity organization society in the United States. In announcing the Biennial Meeting, Clark W. Blackburn, the newly appointed general director of the Association, said:

> This anniversary occasion can serve as a vantage point from which we can gain heightened perspective. Looking backward to the early beginnings of this important movement in the growth of social work, we can measure to some extent the distance we have traveled and the advances we have made. No period in history has equaled the past seventy-five years in the degree and rapidity of social change, and in the severity of shocks and dislocations to which all social institutions, including the family, have been exposed. In this period, family service agencies have emerged as a strong social force, contributing to the development of a major profession while retaining the vigor of a voluntary citizen movement.[1]

At the dinner meeting, the Association and the local agency paid brief tribute to some of the early leaders of the movement. Brooks Potter of Boston,* then president of the Board of Directors of the Association, reviewed the highlights of Mary E. Richmond's career

---

* Earlier in 1952, Brooks Potter had been nominated—and was subsequently elected—president of the National Conference of Social Work for the year 1953–54.

169

and pointed to her influence on social work development. In appraising her contribution, Mr. Potter said:

> When we contemplate the present-day functioning of a family service agency adhering to the standards of our national association, is it not truly amazing that this one woman, by the sheer force of her own self-propelled will and self-acquired education, could have left such an indelible mark on one of the great fields of social endeavor in a democracy? Truly this is a case where it can be said that all the darkness in the world cannot put out the light of one small candle.[2]

The program of the Biennial followed the usual pattern of assessing current problems and of considering ways of meeting them. The subjects discussed at the general sessions reflected the continuing concern of the Association for strengthening the family and its constant search for new knowledge to achieve this end. Among the speakers were Dr. Martha M. Eliot, chief of the Children's Bureau, who discussed the needs and opportunities of the family[3] and Leonard S. Cottrell, Jr., of the Russell Sage Foundation, who reported on new directions for research on the American family.[4]

At the meeting of the General Assembly, Mrs. Malcolm J. Edgerton presented the report of the Committee on Social Policy, which outlined social principles for the family field and means of implementing them. The General Assembly adopted the statement and authorized the appointment of a public issues committee.[5]

Program Activities

Following the 1952 Biennial Meeting, the Executive Committee appointed a Committee on Public Issues. It received its charge in 1953 and began its work in September of that year, under the chairmanship of Robert H. McConnell of Danville, Virginia, who was later succeeded by Sidney Hollander of Baltimore. This Committee prepared several policy statements on social security, on housing, on needs in defense-impacted communities, on unemployment, and on public assistance.

The Committee also undertook to develop closer relationships with various departments and branches of the federal government, such as the Department of Health, Education, and Welfare and

170

the Social Security Administration, as well as with national organizations whose interests paralleled those of the Association.[6]

The work of the United Community Defense Services unit of the Association, which had begun in April, 1952, increased during the next few years in spite of the cessation of hostilities in Korea. This unit continued its services until the fall of 1955, when it became necessary to cease operations because of the withdrawal of UCDS funds.

During its period of operation, the FSAA-UCDS staff visited a total of 121 different communities and had correspondence with 50 others. The communities visited were alike in that none had a family service agency and all were suffering from the impact of defense activities; they had very little in the way of social service outside the public welfare department and, usually, a county Red Cross unit. In size and location, however, there were wide variations, from a county in New York State with a population of one million to a town of four thousand in Texas.

The field consultants worked closely with county and state departments and with the UCDS field staff of the other national agencies. They kept their focus on the casework field and what it had to offer, rather than on any specific type of agency; thus they were able to work out a wide variety of experimental approaches, such as arranging for a "traveling" social worker to cover several communities, extending existing services to cover a broader area through outpost offices, strengthening public agency facilities, or combining needed services in one organization.[7]

In one instance the FSAA-UCDS unit undertook to organize and administer a casework agency. This agency covered three counties —Pike, Jackson, and Ross—in southern Ohio, where the Atomic Energy Commission was planning a billion and a quarter dollar plant. This construction meant the influx of a labor force of 25,000, many workers bringing their families with them. Existing health and group work services were not adequate to meet the needs of the people already living in the area and there was not one professional caseworker available. Several national agencies associated with UCDS offered recreational and group work services. All agencies agreed that a casework program was needed, and FSAA-UCDS

171

established a casework agency to give service to residents and new-comers in the three counties.

Relationships with lay people and lay sponsorship were built county by county. An area board and three county advisory com-mittees were set up and a staff of two workers engaged, with the understanding that UCDS would provide FSAA with funds to carry the agency for two years and that the area would take over at the end of that time. In addition to giving needed services, this project had value in demonstrating how such service can be developed on an area basis, how area financing can be carried out, and how outpost services can best be given.[8]

Early in 1953 the Personnel Committee of the Association, which had been inactive since 1951, was reorganized with Sidney J. Berkowitz, of the Jewish Family Service Association of Cleveland, as chairman. Subcommittees undertook to prepare guides for the family field on salary scales, personnel practices, and job classifica-tions and evaluations. Another subcommittee and the staff of personnel service gave special attention to recruitment and scholar-ships, working closely with the Council on Social Work Education and other national organizations. In December, 1954, the Board approved the establishment of an FSAA Fellowship Fund, as a means of supplementing the fellowship programs of local agencies.

Because of the increased use of psychiatric consultation by mem-ber agencies, interest was expressed in having the Association de-velop guides for the field. In 1953, a Committee on Psychiatric Consultation, with Perry B. Hall, of the Pittsburgh Family and Children's Service as chairman, agreed to study current practice and to suggest the general direction in which such consultation should develop. The Committee presented its report to the Board in De-cember, 1955, and it was subsequently published by the Association.[9]

The 1954 Biennial Meeting was held in Los Angeles, California, in connection with the seventy-fifth celebration of the founding of the Jewish Family Service of Los Angeles. This was the first time the Biennial Meeting had been held on the West Coast. Sol Morton Isaac of Columbus, Ohio, president of the Board of Directors, opened the conference with an address on "Unhappy Living: Its Challenge to the Family Service Agency." In describing the role and function of the family agency, he listed five specific goals:

1. To establish and to preserve high standards of social work in the field of family service;
2. To disseminate the ever-increasing knowledge of family life in America and to continue the education both of ourselves and of the public;
3. To promote better training for social workers and a more abundant personnel;
4. To correlate through research the vast experience of the past in order to produce better results at less cost;
5. To lead our communities and our nation toward the development of sound social welfare, compatible with our democratic heritage and utilizing all the vast resources of our land, economic and spiritual, public and private.[10]

Other sessions of the Biennial were also devoted to the study of the functions of the family agency in a period of social change and stress. Among the subjects discussed were the needs of growing communities, the relation between family agencies and mental health clinics, and the implications of the recent Association report on *Scope and Methods*.[11]

Review Committee

In December, 1953, the Board of the Association authorized the appointment of a Review Committee to study the activities of the Association and to make recommendations on its structure, services, and budget. Hugh R. Jones of Utica was named chairman and Mrs. Victor H. Shaw of Fairmont, West Virginia, co-chairman.

The Committee, with the help of several subcommittees, formulated a number of questions about the activities of the Association which were submitted to the membership for discussion and opinion. Both board members and professional staff of member agencies participated in the study process, many sending in letters of comment in addition to filling in the questionnaire.

The Review Committee found that, in general, member agencies approved of the program activities carried on by the national staff and by Association committees. Many expressed interest in having the Association expand its program, but there was recognition that such expansion was not feasible with present financial resources.

173

Particular interest was expressed in the further development of informal study projects and of research; a number of subjects were suggested, with a high priority given to treatment of marital problems, casework with children, and casework with the aged. Research on a number of administrative subjects was also suggested. Member agencies expressed interest, too, in the extension of Association activities in the area of professional education.

The report of the Review Committee was submitted to the Board of Directors in May, 1955. The Board accepted the recommendations for expansion of the Association's program and recognized the need to seek funds to make such expansion possible.

Setting New Sights

In July, 1955, Hugh R. Jones was elected president of the Board of Directors and was faced with the responsibility for implementing the recommendations of the Committee he had chaired. At the December, 1955, meeting of the Board, consideration was given to ways of securing income to supplement membership dues so that some of the program activities outlined by the Review Committee might get under way. The Board approved the appointment of an Ad Hoc Development Committee, with Mrs. Victor H. Shaw of Fairmont, West Virginia, as chairman, to outline immediate and long-range goals for Association development.

The range of the Association's on-going activities for the year 1955 is reflected in the following list of committees: Executive; Nominating; Budget and Finance; Membership; Public Issues; Editorial Advisory to *Social Casework*; *Highlights* Advisory; Case Record Exhibit; Personnel; Public Relations; Lawyer–Family Agency Co-operation; Fellowships Fund; Psychiatric Consultation; 1956 Biennial Planning. In addition, there were six Regional Committees: Middle Atlantic, Midwestern, North Atlantic, Pacific Northwest, Pacific Southwest, and Southern.

At the end of 1955, Mr. Jones sent a letter to member agencies, addressed to the president of the board, as well as to General Assembly delegates, in which he highlighted the growth of Association activities, pointed to the urgency of current problems, and suggested ways for the Association to secure increased support. He said, in part, in his Year-End Letter:

174

The year-end business forecasts have carried a common note of high optimism. The whole nation finds assurance in the $387 billion national output reached in 1955. In terms of family welfare, this undoubtedly means that never before have so many American families realized such a large amount of their material wants. This is true even though we know that there are serious economic needs remaining among millions of families living on marginal income, small pensions, or public assistance grants.

It is not a paradox that in a time of wide prosperity family service agencies have been increasingly sought out for help with personal and family difficulties, for the satisfaction of material wants is never the full answer to the problems of human relations. In fact, industrial expansion itself may contribute new social complexities, such as the increased mobility of families. Whatever the origins, all of us know enough of the extent of family conflict, mental illness, delinquency, and maladjustment to realize that our agencies face great challenges.

More people may be availing themselves of family service simply because our field has made itself better known, understood, and accepted. But even with prosperity and greater public approval, our field is feeling the impact of another tremendous factor—simple population growth. In twenty years our population has swelled by 36 million. Now a country of 166 million people, there will be 185 or 190 million Americans in ten more years. We are having ever more children and teenagers, ever more people over sixty-five. There are millions more people within close access to our existing family agencies; millions of others have been on the march to suburbia and to new communities where insistent demands for new agencies are arising. . . .

In a very high proportion of our member agencies today, services given are close to capacity of staff. Nearly a quarter have had to establish waiting lists for appointments. The fact is that many agencies report to us they find it difficult or impossible to be geared to present needs. Under these circumstances how well prepared in our field are we to meet the stepped-up demands in the next decade?

The lower enrolments in schools of social work in recent years make the situation even more urgent. Inability to obtain staff is threatening the very existence of some of our smaller agencies. Much as we shall need more engineers and teachers in the next decade we shall also need more social workers—some 50,000 of them. It is not too much to say that the welfare of the country requires that social work shall not be outdistanced by other professions in attracting young people. . . .

Except for withering on the vine, steady, sufficient growth is the only alternative for the family service field. In view of the proud history of family service in serving the needs of American families and in the development of the profession of social work, there is no question as to which alternative we can accept.[12]

The "proud history" of which Mr. Jones speaks may turn out to be only a prologue to greater accomplishments yet to come. In this 1955 message to the membership, the Association president reveals the same convictions about the importance of family social work and the same belief in people that have characterized the lay

175

leaders since the launching of the early charity organization societies. With such leadership, there can be no "withering on the vine."

References

1. Clark W. Blackburn, "Buffalo, 1952—A Vantage Point," *Family Service Highlights*, Vol. XIII, No. 8 (1952), pp. 113–114.
2. Brooks Potter, "The Long View: A Tribute to a Social Work Pioneer." Address given at 1952 Biennial Meeting, Family Service Association of America. Unpublished.
3. Martha M. Eliot, M.D., "The Family Today: Its Needs and Opportunities," *Social Casework*, Vol. XXXIV, No. 2 (1953), pp. 47–54.
4. Leonard S. Cottrell, Jr., "New Directions for Research on the American Family," *Social Casework*, Vol. XXXIV, No. 2 (1953), pp. 54–60.
5. "F.S.A.A. Adopts Social Principles," *Family Service Highlights*, Vol. XIII, No. 10 (1952), pp. 153–155.
6. "A Stronger Voice in Family Welfare Urged," *Family Service Highlights*, Vol. XVII, No. 3 (1956), pp. 33–37.
7. "Report to the UCDS Field Service Committee on Conclusions and Recommendations of the UCDS Workshop Held September 19–23, 1955," United Community Defense Services, New York, 1955.
8. Alvin L. Schorr, "Mobile Family Living," *Social Casework*, Vol. XXXVII, No. 4 (1956), pp. 175–180; also Alvin L. Schorr, "A Three-County Approach to Casework Service," *Family Service Highlights*, Vol. XVI, No. 7 (1955), pp. 103–106.
9. *Psychiatric Consultation in the Family Service Agency*, Report of the Committee on Psychiatric Consultation, Family Service Association of America, New York, 1956.
10. Sol Morton Isaac, "Unhappy Living: Its Challenge to the Family Service Agency," *Family Service Highlights*, Vol. XV, No. 9 (1954), pp. 131–132.
11. *Scope and Methods of the Family Service Agency*, Report of the Committee on Methods and Scope, Family Service Association of America, New York, 1953.
12. Hugh R. Jones. Letter sent to membership February 28, 1956.

Appendix

Names of the Association from its Founding in 1911

1911: National Association of Societies for Organizing Charity
1912: American Association of Societies for Organizing Charity
1917: American Association for Organizing Charity
1919: American Association for Organizing Family Social Work
1930: Family Welfare Association of America
1946: Family Service Association of America

Charter Members, National Association of Societies for Organizing Charity, 1911

Albany, New York
  Society for the Co-operation of
    Charities
Atlanta, Georgia
  Associated Charities
Atlantic City, New Jersey
  Organized Charities
Baltimore, Maryland
  Federated Charities
Bloomfield, New Jersey
  League for Friendly Service
Bloomington, Illinois
  Bureau of Associated Charities
Boston, Massachusetts
  Associated Charities
Bronxville, New York
  Eastchester Relief Association
Brooklyn, New York
  Bureau of Charities

Buffalo, New York
  Charity Organization Society
Cambridge, Massachusetts
  Associated Charities
Chattanooga, Tennessee
  Associated Charities
Chicago, Illinois
  United Charities
Cincinnati, Ohio
  Associated Charities
Cleveland, Ohio
  Associated Charities
Colorado Springs, Colorado
  Associated Charities
Columbus, Ohio
  Associated Charities
Denver, Colorado
  Charity Organization Society
Des Moines, Iowa
  Associated Charities

Detroit, Michigan
Associated Charities

Elizabeth, New Jersey
Charity Organization Society

Elmira, New York
Social Service League

Erie, Pennsylvania
Bureau of Charities

Fort Worth, Texas
United Charities

Harrisburg, Pennsylvania
Associated Charities

Hartford, Connecticut
Charity Organization Society

Indianapolis, Indiana
Charity Organization Society

Jacksonville, Florida
Associated Charities

Kalamazoo, Michigan
Charity Organization Department
Women's Civic Improvement
League

Lancaster, Pennsylvania
Charity Society

Lawrence, Massachusetts
City Mission

Los Angeles, California
Associated Charities

Milwaukee, Wisconsin
Associated Charities

Minneapolis, Minnesota
Associated Charities

Newark, New Jersey
Bureau of Associated Charities

New Britain, Connecticut
Charity Organization

Newburgh, New York
Associated Charities

Newport, Rhode Island
Charity Organization Society

New York, New York
Charity Organization Society

Paterson, New Jersey
Charity Organization Society

Pensacola, Florida
Associated Charities

Philadelphia, Pennsylvania
Society for Organizing Charity

Phoenix, Arizona
Associated Charities

Pittsburgh, Pennsylvania
Associated Charities

Portland, Oregon
Associated Charities

Providence, Rhode Island
Society for Organizing Charity

St. Louis, Missouri
Provident Association

Salem, Massachusetts
Associated Charities

Savannah, Georgia
Associated Charities

Seattle, Washington
Charity Organization Society

Somerville, Massachusetts
Associated Charities

South Bend, Indiana
Associated Charities

Spokane, Washington
Associated Charities

Springfield, Massachusetts
Union Relief Association

Stamford, Connecticut
Associated Charities

Syracuse, New York
Associated Charities

Toledo, Ohio
Federation of Charities

Washington, D. C.
Associated Charities

Waterbury, Connecticut
Charity Organization Society

Wheeling, West Virginia
Associated Charities

Worcester, Massachusetts
Associated Charities

Youngstown, Ohio
Charity Organization Society

Number of Agencies in the Association Membership

1911	62	1935	244
1912	84	1945	228
1913	102	1955	249
1914	143		(plus 8 Pre-Member
1915	144		Affiliates)
1925	220		

Presidents of the Board of Directors of the Association

(From 1911 to 1924 the president was called the chairman
of the Executive Committee)

1911–1914: John F. Moors, Boston, Massachusetts
1914–1920: Mrs. William H. Lothrop, Boston, Massachusetts
Sept.-Oct., 1920: Lawson Purdy, New York, New York (Acting)
1920–1936: Mrs. John M. Glenn, New York, New York
1936–1939: Stanley P. Davies, New York, New York
1939–1942: Laurence M. Williams, New Orleans, Louisiana
1943–1947: Ralph A. Uihlein, Milwaukee, Wisconsin
1947–1953: Brooks Potter, Boston, Massachusetts
1953–1955: Sol Morton Isaac, Columbus, Ohio
1955–   : Hugh R. Jones, Utica, New York

General Directors of the Association

(Known variously as general secretary, executive director, and so on)

1911–1919: Francis H. McLean
Oct., 1919–May, 1920: Thomas K. Brown
1920–1925: David H. Holbrook
1925–1946: Linton B. Swift
1946–1951: Frank J. Hertel
1951–1952: Earl N. Parker (Acting)
1952–   : Clark W. Blackburn

Index

A

Administration of Relief in Unemployment Emergencies, The, 115
Aged, 136, 159
Agency dues, *see* Financial support of national association
Aid to dependent children, 67–70
Albany, N. Y., Society for the Co-operation of Charities, 177
Allegheny County agencies, iii, 69
Almoners, 26
Almsgiving, 3–15, 17, 32; *see also* Private relief, Public relief, Relief
Almy, Frederic, 58, 64, 68, 73, 82
American Association for Community Organization, 107
American Association for Organizing Charity, 73, 83n, 96, 177
American Association for Organizing Family Social Work, 52, 83n, 96, 177
American Association of Social Workers, 102, 121, 141
American Association of Societies for Organizing Charity, 72, 83n, 177
American Charities, 46
American Federation of International Institutes, 148
American Federation of Labor, 149
American National Red Cross, 102, 147; *see also* Red Cross Home Service
American Public Welfare Association, 119, 135
American Social Science Association, 11
American War-Community Services (AWCS), 148–149, 151, 153, 162, 165
Annual Meeting of the Association: 1912, 91; 1918, 74, 92; 1919, 94, 96; 1921, 100; 1922, 101; 1929, 112; 1930, 109; 1931, 115; 1935, 130; 1938, 137
Armed forces, social workers in, 148
Associated Charities, *see* name of specific city
Association, the national: early history, 52, 72, 73, 76–93, 95; founding, 83,
177; general directors, viii, 85, 96, 102, 108, 119, 126, 147, 156, 169, 179; membership, 84, 179; names, 83n, 96, 158, 177; organization and administration, 96, 151, 152; presidents, viii, 104, 137, 145, 147, 169, 172, 174, 179; relations with Charity Organization Department, 85; relations with federal government, 165, 170; relations with other organizations, 101, 102, 119, 143, 145, 147, 153, 165, 170; review committee to study the, 173, 174; and sectarian agencies, 91; *see also* Annual Meeting of the Association, Biennial Meeting of the Association, Committees of the Association, Membership requirements, and so on
Associations for Improving the Condition of the Poor, vi, 6
Atlanta, Ga., Associated Charities, 177
Atlantic City, N. J., Organized Charities, 177
Atomic Energy Commission project, 171
Ayres, Philip W., 45

B

Babcock, Rev. Maltbie, 26
Bachman, Rev. J. W., vi, 11, 28
Baltimore: Federated Charities, 177; pioneer workers in, vii, 33, 40, 41, 47, 57
Baltimore Charity Organization Society, 26, 31, 40, 46, 47, 114
Basic Concepts in Casework Practice, Committee to Study, 160
Bedford, Caroline, 111
Berkowitz, Sidney J., 172
Biennial Meeting of the Association: first, 130; 1946, 156, 158; 1948, 160; 1950, 163; 1952, 166, 169, 170; 1954, 172, 173
Birtwell, Mary L., 67
Blackburn, Clark W., iii, 169, 179

180

Meetings, *see* Annual Meeting of the Association, Biennial Meeting of the Association, Conference, and so on
Membership: growth of, 179; individual, 126; Mothers Assistance Funds, 91; pre-member affiliates, 162, 179; and public departments, 91, 99, 100, 112; sectarian agencies, 91
Membership Committee, 89–91, 138, 162
Membership requirements, 89–91, 99, 100, 126, 137, 138, 162
Mental Health, International Congress of, 165
Mergers, 151
Methods and Scope, Committee on, 167
Meyer, Dr. Adolph, 53
Milford Conference, 95, 102–104
Military service: casework problems arising from, 143, 146; of social workers, 148
Milwaukee: Associated Charities, 178; family agency and relief, 122; pioneer leader, 12
Minneapolis: agency staff, 104, 156, 160; Associated Charities, 178; Family Welfare Association, 156
Misery and Its Causes, 48
Monthly Summaries, on unemployment relief, 116, 117, 122, 123
Montreal Charity Organization Society, executive, 71
Moors, John F., 179
Morse, Frances R., 7, 17, 18, 33, 44, 61
Mothers' aid legislation, 67–70
Mothers Assistance Funds, membership eligibility, 91

N

Names: of agencies, 6, 8, 9, 95, 96, 137, 158, 177; of the Association, 83n, 96, 158, 177
National Association of Social Workers, 102; *see also* American Association of Social Workers
National Association of Societies for Organizing Charity, 52, 71, 83, 177; *see also* Association, the national
National Board of the Young Women's Christian Association, 149
National Conference of Charities and Correction: beginning of, 11; by date, 1879, 24; 1880, 60; 1881, 59; 1883, vi, 20; 1887, 57; 1888, 19; 1889, 57; 1890, 63, 77; 1891, 77; 1892, vi, 61; 1896, 42; 1897, 25, 43, 44, 63; 1902, 90n; 1903, 65; 1905, 78; 1907, 80;

1908, 48; 1909, 82; 1912, 68; Committee on Charity Organization, 11, 12, 20, 24, 38, 38n, 40, 76–78, 90n; Committee on Needy Families in Their Homes, 90n; Committee on the Prevention of Pauperism, 58
National Conference of Social Work: beginning of, 11; 1931, 111; 1953–54, 169n; *see also* National Conference of Charities and Correction
National Consumers' League, 27
National Council on Social Work Education, 165
National defense program, 144–154
National Organization for Public Health Nursing, 149
National Recreation Association, 31
National Social Welfare Assembly, 102, 149, 165
National Social Work Council, 102, 114n, 143, 147, 149
National Urban League, 149
Nelson, Robert F., 166
New Alignments Between Public and Private Agencies, 126, 127
New Britain, Conn., Charity Organization, 178
New charity, *see* Scientific charity
New Haven Organized Charities Association, 7, 24
New York: beginning of settlement work, 46; early agencies, 5, 6, 9, 27, 63; public relief in, 59, 63; registration bureau, 6, 17, 18
New York agencies, lay leaders and staffs of, vii, 9, 12, 18, 21, 22, 23, 27, 31, 35, 39, 41, 45, 46, 57, 58, 66, 80, 95, 145, 150
New York Association for Improving the Condition of the Poor, 6
New York Charity Organization Society, 10, 16, 21, 26, 27, 28, 29, 39, 41, 45, 51, 57, 63, 64, 66, 78n, 81, 95, 117, 178
New York Community Service Society, iv, viii, 145; *see also* New York Charity Organization Society
New York Evening Post, 21, 114
New York Jewish Family Service, 146, 160
New York School of Social Work of Columbia University, 45, 46, 81, 97, 98, 114
New York State Board of Charities, 9
New York State Charities Aid Association, 9, 63
New York United Hebrew Charities, 9

Social insurance, 68, 131
Social Policy, Association, Committee on, 166, 170; *see also* Public Issues
Social reforms, 4, 6, 23–31
Social Security: Act, 131; Administration, 171; Board, 131
Social service exchange, 19, 73; *see also* Registration bureaus
Social Welfare, Advisory Committee on, 147
Social Welfare Assembly, National, 102, 149, 165
Social Work Education, Council on, 172; *see also* Professional education
Social work literature, development of, 46–48, 53, 79, 96, 97, 104, 149–151; *see also* Publications
Social Work Vocational Bureau, iii, 143, 159, 165
Social Workers, National Association of, 102; *see also* American Association of Social Workers
Societies for the Prevention of Pauperism, vi, 5, 6
Somerville, Mass., Associated Charities, 178
South Bend, Ind., Associated Charities, 178
Spokane, Wash., Associated Charities, 178
Springfield, Mass., Union Relief Association, 178
Staff development, *see* Professional training
Stamford, Conn.: Associated Charities, 178; Family and Children's Services, 160
Statistical forms, development of, 12, 77, 81
Statistics: of family casework, 162; and Information Service, Committee on, 135; and Studies, Committee on, 162
Statistics Department, Russell Sage Foundation, 108, 162
Studies and Information, Department of, 135, 136, 162; *see also* Information Service
Studies of public departments, 73
Support of Family Social Work, Committee on, 152; *see also* Financial support of national association
Survey, The, 46, 70, 78n
Surveys, community, 71, 73, 81, 87
Swift, Linton B., 108, 119, 120, 126, 127, 143, 147, 155, 156, 179
Syracuse Associated Charities, 7, 178

T

Taft, Charles P., 147
Teaching records, 49, 52, 81, 104, 120, 151; *see also* Case record exhibit
Temporary Emergency Relief Administrations, 119
Tenements, *see* Housing, Social reforms
Time to Plan Is Now, The, 108, 111
Titles of agencies, *see* Names of agencies
Toledo, Ohio: Federation of Charities, 178; Social Service Federation, 117; unemployment crisis, 109, 110, 117, 118
Towle, Charlotte, 163, 165
Training, Committee on, 104; *see also* Professional training
"Trampery," *see* Vagrancy
Transients and Homeless, 113–114; *see also* Homeless
Transportation Agreement, 30, 77, 85, 90
Truesdale, G. C., 12
Tuberculosis, committee on prevention of, 29
Tuckerman, Joseph, vi, 6, 33

U

Uihlein, Ralph A., 147, 179
Unemployment: committees on, 108–112, 114; conferences on, 101, 119; national action on, 114, 119; pamphlets on, 108, 111, 115; periods of, 100, 101, 107–123
United Charities, *see* name of specific city
United Community Defense Services (UCDS), 164, 171, 172
United Defense Fund, 164
United Hebrew Charities of New York, 9
United Jewish Charities in Chicago, 68
U. S. Committee for the Care of European Children, 143
Uzzell, Mabel, 134, 143

V

Vagrancy, 7, 29, 30
Vaile, Gertrude, vii, 71, 72, 99, 104
Van Kleeck, Mary, 101
Veterans Administration, 147
Visiting housekeepers, *see* Homemakers
Visiting nurse association, 29
Vocational guidance, 144